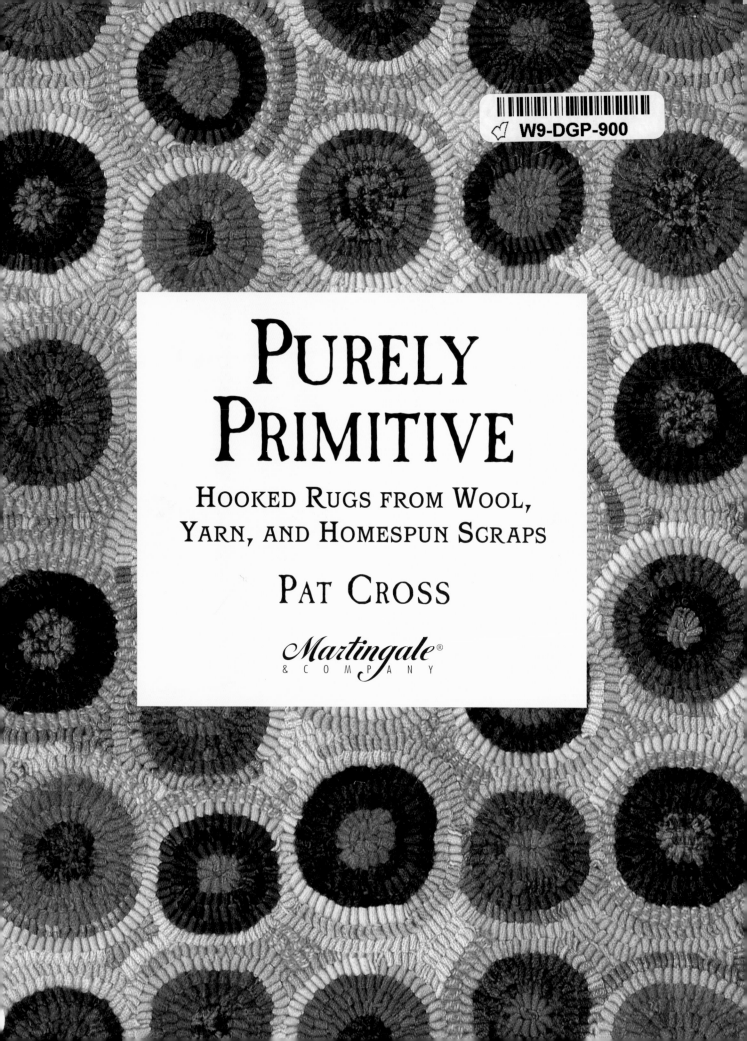

W9-DGP-900

PURELY PRIMITIVE

HOOKED RUGS FROM WOOL, YARN, AND HOMESPUN SCRAPS

PAT CROSS

Martingale®
& COMPANY

That Patchwork Place® is an imprint
of Martingale & Company®.

Purely Primitive: Hooked Rugs from
Wool, Yarn, and Homespun Scraps
© 2003 by Pat Cross

Martingale & Company
20205 144th Avenue NE
Woodinville, WA 98072-8478 USA
www.martingale-pub.com

Credits

President .... Nancy J. Martin
CEO .... Daniel J. Martin
Publisher .... Jane Hamada
Editorial Director .... Mary V. Green
Managing Editor .... Tina Cook
Technical Editor .... Ellen Pahl
Copy Editor .... Ellen Balstad
Design Director... Stan Green
Illustrator.. Robin Strobel
Cover & Text Designer .... Shelly Garrison
Photographer.. Brent Kane
Location photos were taken at the home of Jerry and
Michele Aalbu in Snohomish, Washington.

No part of this product may be reproduced in any form,
unless otherwise stated, in which case reproduction is limited to the use of the purchaser. The written instructions,
photographs, designs, projects, and patterns are intended
for the personal, noncommercial use of the retail purchaser and are under federal copyright laws; they are not to be
reproduced by any electronic, mechanical, or other means,
including informational storage or retrieval systems, for
commercial use. Permission is granted to photocopy patterns for the personal use of the retail purchaser.

The information in this book is presented in good
faith, but no warranty is given nor results guaranteed.
Since Martingale & Company has no control over choice
of materials or procedures, the company assumes no
responsibility for the use of this information.

Printed in China
08 07 06 05 04 03   8 7 6 5 4 3 2 1

Library of Congress Cataloging-in-Publication Data

Cross, Pat
    Purely primitive: hooked rugs from wool, yarn, and
homespun scraps / Pat Cross.
        p. cm.
    ISBN 1-56477-486-4
1. Rugs, Hooked. I. Title.
    TT850.C75 2003
    746.7'4--dc22
                                              2003016701

Mission Statement
Dedicated to providing quality products
and service to inspire creativity.

Dedication

To my husband, Tom. With his constant, unconditional love and support, I have attended many rug camps, purchased hundreds of yards of wool, and had the freedom to do and explore the art I love. We have similar passions and respect each other's interests. He cuts up wood to make antique-looking furniture while I cut up wool to make primitive hooked rugs.

Acknowledgments

Throughout my twelve years in rug hooking, I have met a lot of people who share my interest. I have taken classes and workshops from many talented people. All of them have influenced me greatly. It would be difficult to acknowledge everyone for fear I'd overlook someone, but there are a few people I want to mention and thank for getting me "hooked":

Mum J., my college housemother, exposed me to my first hooked rug. Joan Moshimer gave me a list of rug-hooking teachers that led me to my first teacher, Genevieve Patterson. Jennifer McKelvie introduced me to dyeing and rug camps. Marion Ham was the director of the first rug-hooking camp I ever attended, Quail Hill, and it was at Marion's camp that my interest in rug hooking became a passion. The Quail Hill experience led me to many camps, but my favorite is the Green Mountain Rug School. At the Green Mountain Rug School, I have been exposed to incredibly talented teachers and students.

CONTENTS

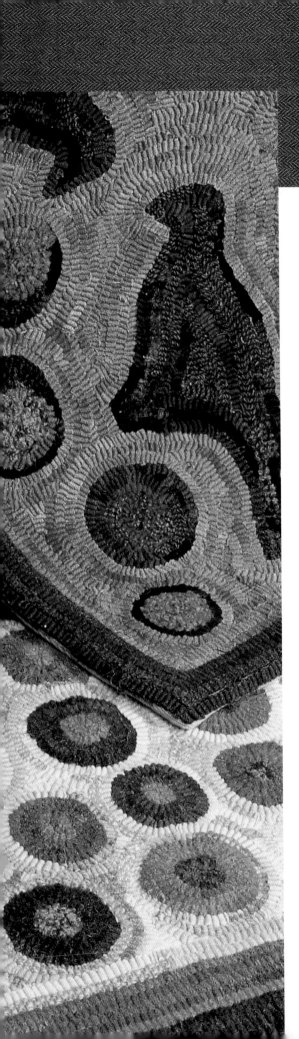

PREFACE

In the past eight years, my husband and I have lived in five states. Throughout all that moving, rug hooking kept me sane; it gave me something constructive to do, something to look forward to, and many opportunities to get out of the house. Those opportunities and my many rug-hooking friends helped get me through that period.

During this time, I decided I would write a book to share the wonderful world of rug hooking with others who haven't been exposed to it or who aren't able to travel or take classes.

After one more move, I'm finally settled. This time I love my house and where I live, and I'm content. Rug hooking makes me happy. There is something very comforting about sitting in my studio, rhythmically pulling up loops and feeling wool between my fingers. My studio is my safe haven where I'm calm and relaxed; my cats gather there and my mind dreams of color, wool, and future rugs.

INTRODUCTION

When our country was young, most people lived simple lives. Their homes were usually very basic and had only the bare essentials. Women didn't have the luxury of going to a local shopping center and buying decorations for their homes. If they wanted to add a bit of color or beauty, most had to make decorations themselves. These women were extremely creative. They designed what they wanted to make and they figured out how to use scraps and leftover materials to bring their projects to life.

Quilts kept the family warm on cold nights and contributed a bit of color to the beds. Rugs added some beauty, warmth, and color to an otherwise plain house. Hooked rugs might adorn the hearth when company came, add warmth to a drafty area, or be set on a table to brighten the home. Our predecessors made the most of what they had and used it wisely.

Early hooked rugs were simple in design. The inspiration for the rug designs often came from items around the home or farm. Popular design subjects were animals, houses, and flowers. The simple, primitive hooked rugs exposed much about the maker's life and feelings, and they are now treasured pieces of the past. The whimsical designs, which often disregarded proportions, are now looked at as true American folk art and catch collectors' eyes. People appreciate the wonderful folk-art rugs of our ancestors and want them for their own homes.

Unfortunately, many of the early hooked rugs did not survive to the present day. Those that remain are quite expensive. Since antique rugs are scarce and their prices are high, many people are trying to re-create them. This book will show you how to make hooked rugs and achieve the wonderful, antique scrappy look found in primitive rugs.

I've also included instructions for dyeing your own wool colors, since wool is not readily available in as many colors as quilting cottons and other fabrics. I've found that many rug hookers enjoy the dyeing process as much as hooking.

Also look for "Hooker's Hints" scattered throughout the book. These are just a few of my extra tips and helpful advice that you may find of interest regarding rug hooking.

WHAT MAKES A RUG PRIMITIVE?

Some say the word *primitive* means simple, untrained, lacking detail or shading, childlike, or crudely done. In this book, *primitive* defines a style, a feeling, and an image that depicts a simpler time. Primitive hooked rugs look old, uncomplicated, and whimsical without being cutesy.

Proportion, or lack of, was another characteristic that seemed to prevail in the wonderful, old primitive rugs of the nineteenth century. You may have found a bird as big as a tree sitting on top of a house. The artists drawing these designs were not trained. Their disregard for proportion and perspective were what added to the charm and character of these early hooked rugs. There was also a scrappy look to the rugs. By this I mean different fabrics and colors were used haphazardly. It makes me wonder if the maker was actually using every scrap available or working at night with poor lighting.

Many of the designs in early hooked rugs were based on familiar items around the home. Animals were very popular, especially horses, birds, cats, and dogs. Flowers appeared in borders or as the focal point in a basket or urn. And the family home— the very house the rug hooker lived in—was often depicted on their rug.

In addition, there were patches of different colors. For example, the background might be black but with a large patch of brown. Did the maker run out of background color? Did an area get wet and the unstable color fade? No one really knows. We can only speculate.

Pat's Definition of Primitive Hooked Rugs

Primitive hooked rugs . . .

- are simple but heartwarming in design.
- are muted, mellow, and rich with color.
- are made of wool, cotton, and linen textiles.
- express, enrich, and share a piece of the past.

A lot of work went into making primitive hooked rugs. It's a shame that more of these wonderful old rugs did not survive. But the art of making them has survived, even though the process has changed. Today we pick up the phone and order our supplies. And many of us love the "hunt" for wool in thrift shops. It's a thrill to find a plaid, pleated skirt in a large size because we know it will yield a couple of yards of wool for only a few dollars. With our finds, we try to produce rugs with colors that mimic the wonderful old muted colors that the early hooked rugs faded to over time.

The rugs that capture my heart are the more simple rugs that date from the mid to late 1800s. They were made in households that couldn't afford expensive imported carpets. These rugs were utilitarian in nature. They mainly provided warmth to the cold, bare floors and a bit of color to the home. Many did not survive simply because they were used. When the rugs became heavily soiled or worn, they were discarded and replaced with newly made ones.

A Little Bit of History

The primitive hooked rugs that we know today date back to the late eighteenth century. It was once thought that these hooked rugs were an invention of the British, but this assumption was discredited after a great deal of research. Evidence of hooked rugs or writings about them have not been found in any museums or private collections in Great Britain. Hooked rugs are actually an American creation. They have even been referred to as "America's one indigenous folk art." When I say American, however, I'm referring to the continent of North America because there is uncertainty regarding whether the first hooked rugs came from Canada's Maritime Provinces or the United States' New England region.

Rugs made in the very late eighteenth century and early nineteenth century were known as "bed ruggs." They were used to cover beds and provide warmth. Bed ruggs usually had a linen base and woolen yarn woven through it. Until about 1820, "rugg" meant a coarse woolen cloth or bedcover.

During the second half of the nineteenth century, Edward Frost began the first rug pattern business. He drew rug-hooking patterns and sold them from his peddler wagon. Later, patterns became a mail-order business through the Montgomery Ward catalog and Ralph Burnham, a noted collector of, and lecturer on, hooked rugs.

Early Improvisation

Early rug hookers were creative when it came to rug supplies. If they couldn't afford new burlap as a backing for their rug, they improvised by using old grain bags that held coffee, sugar, or feed. Burlap as we know it was also called gunny or Hessian cloth. It was introduced to Europe from India around 1820. By 1850, British mills were producing it for commercial use and began exporting it. Rug hookers occasionally used linen as a backing, but it was expensive and the tight weave of the linen made it difficult to use. As a result, burlap was the most common backing found on the early hooked rugs.

After finding suitable backing material, the rug hooker drew a design. They usually drew with a piece of charcoal—a cold ember from the fireplace. The rug hook was nothing more than a bent nail embedded into a piece of wood that served as the handle.

Rug-hooking fabrics became another challenge. Most of the individuals who hooked these simple, primitive rugs were not rich. Families of wealth had carpets that were made in Asia or Turkey. Rug hookers used fabric they could spare. An old wool shawl, used blankets, outgrown and recycled children's clothes, cotton quilt scraps, or even a tired work dress were pulled out of the scrap bag. Old military uniforms were also used.

The poem at right, whose author is unknown, was found in a New England attic and was often used by collector Ralph Burnham in his lectures in the 1930s.

Nuts for dyeing, old burlap, feedsacks, a homemade hook, a piece of charcoal, an old wool blanket, scraps of wool and cotton—these are the supplies creative women of the past might have used to make their rugs.

The Revolutionary Hooked Rug

When Dad came back from Bunker Hill
And the Colonies were free,
He hung his musket over the shelf
And his sword on the saddle tree.

His officer's coat and his soiled buff vest
His pants and his mufflings snug
He lovingly laid on Granma's lap,
With his old red mitts and his woolen cap,
To be put in a grand hooked rug.

The rug was hooked on a linen ground,
With a border of roses red,
And there and here it was splashed with
     a tear
For her boy that had fought and bled.

Lexington, Concord, and Valley Forge,
     'till Monmouth's bloody fight,
'Twas there he fell in a fire of hell,
When Victory was in sight.

We have cherished that rug for many
     a year,
No foot on its flowers would tread,
'Twas Granma's monument to her boy,
Who for liberty fought and bled."

—Author unknown

13

Bright and cheery colors were highly sought after by early rug hookers. Nuts, berries, roots, flowers, and leaves were gathered and used to dye the fabrics. Popular colors were reds, browns, blacks, khakis, and blues. Some colors were very bright and there is evidence of this on the backside of old rugs. The exposed colors on the top faded because the natural dyes weren't colorfast, but the fabric colors on the backside retained their brightness.

There is a theory that the reds found in many of the early hooked rugs came from men's long johns, but this is not true. Men's long johns were not invented until 1909. The red in hooked rugs made prior to 1909 came from other red fabric.

Hooker's Hint

Always roll a rug. Never fold it. Roll it so that the top or right side of the rug is to the outside, just the opposite of what you think, as shown below. Rolling textiles prevents creases and puts less stress on the backing.

PLAIN AND FANCY TOOLS

Rug-hooking tools can be simple and inexpensive or complex and expensive. There are three basic tools you need to make a rug. You need a hoop or a frame to hold the backing taut while you do the actual hooking. You need something to cut the fabric into strips. And you need a hook to pull the loops up through the backing.

Many years ago, your options regarding these three items were few and the choices simple. The art of rug hooking has exploded in the past several years and the choices seem endless now. If this is your very first attempt at rug hooking, try to use items you already have before you invest in expensive tools. If you have none of the tools, buy the least expensive ones or see if you can borrow what you need.

When you find you are really "hooked" on this art, take the time to explore the tools available today. Hooks, frames, and cutters are personal. What works for one person may not be right for you. Don't think the most expensive tool is necessarily the best either. If you select what is best for you and buy quality, you will make a good investment.

Hoops or Frames

When I teach beginners, I tell them to bring a 14"-diameter wooden quilting hoop (not an embroidery hoop). Quilting hoops can be found very easily and are inexpensive. A hoop holds your backing taut. You can rest it in your lap and against a table, leaving both hands free to hook.

You can also use hoops that are mounted on bases, allowing you to sit comfortably with the hoop in your lap. They even collapse or come apart for easy travel.

Quilting Hoop

Rug-hooking frames can be as simple as nailing four slats of wood together to form a square or rectangle. You can then use thumbtacks to hold your backing taut in the opening. You can lean the frame against a table, or attach it to legs and you have a floor frame.

More elaborate frames have metal prongs or gripper strips. They hold the backing in place and thumbtacks aren't needed. Many manufacturers make various frames with gripper strips, including floor frames, lap frames, and collapsible frames, and they come in different sizes.

Puritan Frame with Gripper Strips

Gruber Quilting Frame with Swivel Base

Hooker's Hint

If you find that you prefer to hook in a quilting hoop, and many rug hookers do, you may want to invest in a good-quality hoop. And you may need to purchase a longer bolt to accommodate the rug you are hooking, especially when working with a ¼"-wide strip (a #8 cut) or larger. The rug can get bulky, and the standard bolts are not long enough to accommodate the bulk. Take the quilting hoop to a hardware store and look for a 6" or longer bolt and a wing nut to fit the hoop.

Every day there seems to be a new rug-hooking frame designed. Find what works for you. It's a matter of personal preference in fit, convenience, and cost. I use three different frames. When I travel, especially by plane, I use a collapsible Pittsburgh frame. It folds down flat and fits in my suitcase. At home I usually use a Puritan frame. I sit in a wing chair and pull the frame into my lap. If I am working on a large rug, I use a floor frame that my husband made.

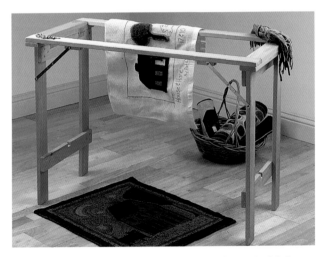

This homemade floor frame uses tacks to hold the rug in place.

Hooker's Hint

Put a pad underneath a rug on the floor. This will keep the rug from slipping and protect it from wear.

Cutters

Cutting your wool into strips requires another tool. Cutters, or wool slitters as some call them, make cutting strips easy. Depending on the size blade you use in the cutter, most cut more than one strip at a time. This saves a great deal of time. If you don't want to use a cutter, you can be a purist and simply tear the fabric by hand or use scissors to cut the fabric. If you're a quilter, you might have a rotary cutter, ruler, and mat, which would also work. Note that cutting a strip narrower than ¼" with scissors or a rotary cutter won't be very easy. All of the rugs in this book use ¼" wool strips. When incorporating cotton homespun, however, I recommend tearing wider strips. See "Hooking with Wool Yarn and Cotton" on page 33.

A Note on Strip-Width Sizes

Rug-hooking strips are referred to by a number that represents $\frac{1}{32}$" increments. For example, a #8 strip is $\frac{8}{32}$" or ¼". A #4 strip is $\frac{4}{32}$" or ⅛". This system was developed by the original strip-cutter manufacturers.

As the demand for cuts wider than ¼" increased, manufacturers added cutter blades and numbers to the sizing system. However, as you will see in the chart below based on American-made cutters, the sizes above #8 do not necessarily correspond directly with $\frac{1}{32}$ of 1". A #8.5, for example, is actually $\frac{10}{32}$"; a #9 is a ⅜" cut ($\frac{12}{32}$"); and a #10 is a ½" cut ($\frac{16}{32}$"). Also note that the Bolivar cutter uses a slightly different numbering system, so be sure to refer to the information that comes with the cutter.

Strip Size	Strip Width
#2	$\frac{2}{32}$"
#3	$\frac{3}{32}$"
#4	$\frac{4}{32}$" (⅛")
#5	$\frac{5}{32}$"
#6	$\frac{6}{32}$" ($\frac{3}{16}$")
#7	$\frac{7}{32}$"
#8	$\frac{8}{32}$" (¼")
#8.5	$\frac{10}{32}$" ($\frac{5}{16}$")
#9	⅜" ($\frac{12}{32}$")
#10	½" ($\frac{16}{32}$")

There are two types of cutters—table-top and clamp. The biggest difference between the two is that the clamp-style models have a handle that makes a larger turning revolution, so you don't have to turn it as many times as the table model. The clamp-style models provide extra stability but also require that you find a place to clamp them to, which can be a disadvantage in some situations.

All cutters come with at least one blade. Different-size cutter blades can be purchased for each cutter, and changing the blades is not difficult.

The Bliss, made by the Harry M. Fraser Company, is a simple table-top model. It uses cutter blades that will cut strips anywhere from $^2/_{32}$" wide (size #2) to $^8/_{32}$" wide (size #8). This is the first cutter I bought. It's a great cutter to travel with because you never have to worry about finding a place to clamp it.

The clamp-style cutters include the Fraser 500-1, Rigby, and Townsend cutters. These cutters can cut strips up to $^1/_2$" wide. The Rigby model can accommodate two different blades at one time. I purchased a Fraser cutter when I started cutting strips in large quantities to assemble kits for students. Its larger handle revolution increased my productivity. The Townsend cutter, which I also own, is new to the rug-hooking world. It is fashioned after the Bolivar, a Canadian-made, clamp-style cutter, but the Townsend is made in the United States and is readily available. It's the Rolls-Royce of cutters. It is a heavy piece of equipment, and it's easy to change the blade (Townsend calls it a cartridge) to cut different-size strips. With the #8 blade, you cut three strips at once, and you turn the handle less to cut the strips. Also, the handle folds, making it easier to transport the cutter in a carrying case.

Townsend Clamp-Style Cutter

Bliss Table-Top Cutter

Hooks

Hooks have come a long way from the bent nail imbedded in a piece of wood that our great-grandmothers used for rug hooking. Today hooks are available in all sizes, shapes, colors, and prices. You can buy a simple Moshimer hook for five dollars or spend up to 10 times that for a beautiful custom-made hook with an exotic-wood handle.

The Moshimer hook is a great little hook that I generally recommend for beginners. It has a small wooden handle and comes in four different sizes—fine, medium, coarse, and primitive. It's inexpensive and fits most hands. Every person's hands are different, and you want a hook that fits your hand comfortably. Consider the handle shape and the weight when choosing.

Start with a lightweight medium or primitive hook for the projects in this book.

As you become more experienced and "hooked" on rug hooking, you can try other hooks. You might consider the high-quality Hartman hooks made in Ireland. They come in several sizes with different-shaped wooden handles and brass hooks. At camps and workshops there are also a variety of hooks available. Test-drive various ones until you discover one that is perfect for you. Finding the right hook for your hand can prevent painful physical problems such as muscle and tendon strain. For example, if you use a fine hook meant for very narrow strips of wool and you're doing primitive rug hooking with wide strips, it is going to be much harder to pull the wider strips up through the backing. If you use a large or heavy handled hook and your hands are small, you may put stress on tendons and muscles.

Some people suggest having a couple of different hooks and switching back and forth. A friend who does woodworking made my favorite hook for me. It is fashioned after the Moshimer hook but made out of cocobola wood. I have small hands and this hook meets my needs. I use it almost exclusively. Again, this is a personal preference, and you have to be comfortable with the hook or hooks you choose.

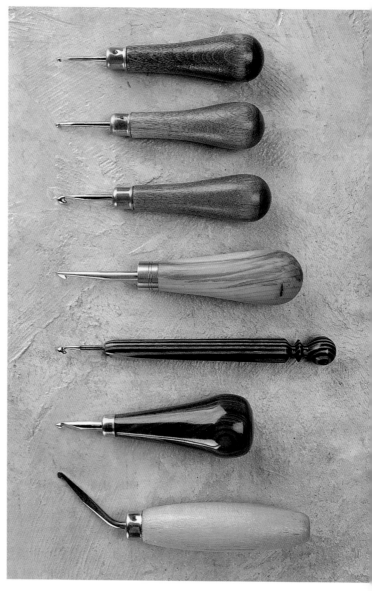

Hooks, from Top to Bottom: Moshimer (Fine), Moshimer (Medium), Moshimer (Coarse), Hartman, Valkyrie, Richie, Rittermere Bent

19

MATERIALS FOR HOOKED RUGS

To hook a rug, you will need a foundation or backing, and fabric strips.

Foundations or Backings

All rugs are hooked by pulling up strips of wool or other fabric through a woven foundation or backing. The terms *foundation* and *backing* are used interchangeably throughout this book. There are four basic backings: burlap, monk's cloth, rug warp, and linen. Scottish burlap, monk's cloth, and primitive linen are the most common backings used for primitive rugs. They can all accommodate the wider strips used in primitive hooking. Rug warp is best used with smaller cut strips. Matching a backing to the strip width helps prevent hand injuries and makes rug hooking much easier.

The burlap sold today is better than the old burlap used in antique rugs, which was unstable and didn't hold up; it was the reason many great old rugs didn't survive. Monk's cloth is 100% even-weave cotton. It's soft and easy to hook on. Linen is the most expensive backing available, and some say it is the most durable.

From left to right: monk's cloth, burlap, and primitive linen are examples of backings used in primitive rug hooking.

Foundations are like hooks and frames; you need to use what you like. Try them all and decide which one you like best. Whatever you use for rug hooking, buy the best you can afford. A good foundation is essential for a good rug. I've tried all the different types of backings and I use Scottish primitive linen exclusively.

Wool, Wonderful Wool

Wool is one of nature's textiles. It is soft, strong, supple, and resilient. It has been around for centuries. In 1800 B.C., the people of the

21

Babylonian civilization distinguished between sheep for food and sheep for wool. As time went on, people learned to appreciate the various wools based on the length of the fiber, fineness, and density. Eventually they learned to manipulate the fibers by hand, twisting, weaving, and blending them into sheets of fabric. By the late eighteenth century, the textile industry was growing, and machines were invented to carry out the process that for centuries had been done by hand. This resulted in factories and a huge industry to satisfy the growing demand for fabrics.

Wool, 100% wool, is the fabric of choice for hooking rugs. The most desirable is flannel-weight wool. Think back to the old pleated wool skirts that many of us wore when we were growing up. A yard of flannel-weight wool weighs about 12 ounces. Gabardine and worsted wools are not recommended because of their texture. They tend to be hard, stiff, and the wrong weight. And most blanket and coat wools are too heavy to use for rug hooking.

Good primitive rug-hooking wools include plaids, herringbones, checks, heathers, and paisleys. Mixtures of coarse and fine-textured wools add great character to primitive rugs. No color is too ugly. Remember, you can always change an ugly color by dyeing. See "Simple Ways to Dye Wool and Get Primitive Colors" on page 39.

Other wools to consider are wool crepe, mohair, and cashmere. Wool crepe is best used in very small quantities. It ravels and doesn't wear well, but sometimes a tiny bit is the perfect accent texture and color. Mohair is another type of wool that adds great texture, but it isn't durable. One-hundred-percent cashmere doesn't wear well, but it does feel good! Wool with some cashmere adds great, rich texture and hooks very easily.

These are great "as is" wools. Each side of the wools offers a different shade and /or texture.

These are wonderful wools to overdye. Notice the texture and variety.

These two "as is" wool pieces can be used together. One is a heather and the other is a herringbone. They were used for the background in Primitive Posies on page 85.

Wool with textures like these are appropriate for design elements such as cabins, tree trunks, and fences.

These "as is" greens will work well as leaves, grasses, vines, centers of flowers, and even backgrounds.

Think pumpkins, vines, fall flowers, and changing leaves when you see a selection of wools like this.

If you're making a large rug that will receive a great deal of use, use 100% wool, and ideally new wool. It's durable and worth the investment for a large project.

Many rug hookers are addicted to the hunt for recycled wool—wool from clothing and other items. Using recycled 100% wool is fine; just be sure not to use any worn portions of a garment. The best recycled wool buys are pleated skirts. Slacks are good, but blazers are a lot of work and don't provide a great deal of useable wool. If it's an absolutely fabulous color, though, don't pass it up. Recycled wool can be a tremendous bargain, but there are a couple extra steps in using recycled wool versus new wool. Recycled wool must be washed, disassembled, and worn areas discarded.

So how do you know if you have 100% wool? Some say you can tell by the way it sounds when you tear it. Others say you'll know by the way it feels and even smells. And some trust the fabric label. However, there are two tests that will tell you if you have 100% wool. The first test is the burn test. Take a couple of threads (one from each direction in the weave) and put a match to them. If it's wool, it will smell like burned hair. The second test is the bleach test. Place a piece of wool about 1" square in a glass dish and cover it with bleach. If it's 100% wool, it will dissolve completely within 24 hours. If there is some fiber left after that time, it's probably a blend of wool and some synthetic.

Wool blends can be used in rug hooking, but keep in mind that blends don't dye well, don't repel dirt, and aren't as resilient as 100%-wool fabrics. Wool blends can also dull the blades on your cutter. Don't let this totally discourage you, but try to limit the blend to no less than 80% wool.

Once you have your wool, wash it before it is used. Recycled wool can be washed before it's taken apart. Some say that new wool doesn't need to be washed, but I make it a general practice to wash it all before I put it in my wool closet. You never know where the wool has been, and washing removes dirt, odors, bugs, and cleaning fluids. Washing also tightens the fibers and fluffs the wool.

The general rule of thumb for machine washing wool is to use a warm wash and a cold rinse. Use a liquid detergent without bleach because the liquid dissolves better than dry detergent. Products such as Tide or Era are good choices. Follow up by throwing the wool into the dryer with a fabric softener sheet. Dry on medium heat.

I have found over the years that the amount of agitation in the washer is what fluffs and tightens the fibers of the wool. If it's very thin wool, try a longer wash cycle. You may even need to wash it twice. If the wool is already a nice weight for rug hooking, try a short or delicate cycle and maybe even a cooler wash. All washing machines are different, so you will need to see how your wool felts up in your machine. If you over-agitate the wool, it may become thick, almost coat weight.

Hooker's Hint

If you're drying a small load of wool, add a dry terry cloth towel to the dryer. The towel will help fluff up the wool and keep the fabrics bouncing around in the dryer, thus leaving few, if any, wrinkles.

When drying wool, be cautious and clean out the dryer lint trap frequently. Wool produces a lot of lint and if you don't clean the trap regularly, it can create a fire hazard.

When you store your wool, keep it away from bright sunlight to prevent fading. Also, if you store it in plastic, keep it in a cool, dry place. You don't want any moisture to accumulate and cause your wool to mildew.

Bulky, Natural Wool Yarn

Bulky, natural wool yarn is another fiber that I use in primitive rug hooking. Bulky wool yarn is about the size of a pencil or your pinkie finger. It isn't dyed but it can be easily. The natural colors range from a dirty white to a dark brown or black. It makes wonderful animals, tree trunks, and fences.

24

Cotton Homespun

Many of the early primitive hooked rugs were hooked with cotton fabrics. The cottons were woven of colored warp and weft, resulting in the same color on each side of the fabric. Today's cotton homespun fabrics are similar to the old woven cottons. The design is the same on the front as on the back. These fabrics are usually found in plaids, stripes, and solids. Cotton fabrics add great texture to rugs, but keep in mind that cotton doesn't repel dirt as easily as wool and isn't as resilient as wool either. Most cotton fabrics are printed with a design on only one side; it's best to avoid using these printed fabrics in hooked rugs.

A Sampling of Cotton Homespuns

Examples of Yarn and Cotton

Floyd: See the photograph on page 66. Look at the body of the cat. Bulky wool yarn was used in the center of his chest and the center of his belly. His whiskers are also natural wool yarn. I used cotton homespun fabrics in the hit-or-miss border, which has a scrappy, multicolor look and includes fabrics used in other parts of the rug.

Tally Ho: See the photograph on page 70. Look for bulky, natural wool yarn on the horse's rump, chest, and near the eye. I used cotton homespun fabrics and yarn throughout the hit-or-miss border.

Primitive Posies: See the photograph below and on page 85. I used cotton homespun fabrics in several of the flowers and throughout the hit-or-miss border.

Old Homestead: See the photograph on page 81. Look at the cat and tree trunk. They are both done entirely with bulky, natural wool yarn in dark brown.

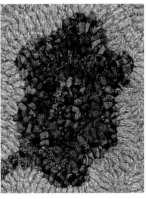

The gold homespun and blue-and-red check shown at left were used in the blue and wavy-edge flowers of Primitive Posies shown above (see page 85 for full-size photo).

25

BASICS OF RUG HOOKING

Once you have the tools, the backing, the wool, and any other fabrics, you're ready to hook your rug. But first you need to prepare the backing and transfer the pattern.

Preparing the Backing

Preparing your foundation or backing properly helps prevent problems later on. Cut a piece of backing that has a minimum of 4" extra on each side. If the finished project is 18" x 30", then you need to cut a piece of backing no smaller than 26" x 38". You need the excess backing so that your pattern fits easily into your hoop or onto your frame.

Serge the outer edges of your backing to prevent it from fraying and raveling. If you don't have a serger, a simple zigzag stitch will do. If you don't have a sewing machine, cover the edges with wide masking tape or duct tape. Folding the

tape in half over the raw edges may look unprofessional but it works, and you will eventually cut off the tape.

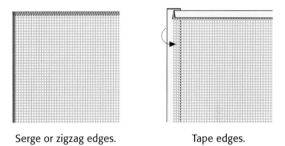

Serge or zigzag edges.　　　Tape edges.

Drawing the Pattern

Drawing your pattern is fun, but you must first make sure that the outer edges of your pattern are drawn on the straight grain of your backing. If you are using monk's cloth or rug warp, this is not a problem since following the grain is very easy. Primitive linen and burlap, however, are looser woven fabrics and it's easy to get off the grain. Some of you may think that you can use a T-square. The problem with that idea is that it may make the pattern look square, but it may not be on the straight of the grain. An inexpensive carpenter's pencil is the miracle tool you can use to draw your pattern on the backing and make sure it is straight. The wide, flat pencil edge fits into the burlap or linen openings very easily.

Measure in from the edge of your backing to where the outside pattern edge should be (about 4"). Place the wide, flat, carpenter's pencil edge into one of the openings in the burlap or linen. While holding the pencil firmly with your right hand (assuming you are right-handed), pull the backing away from you with your left hand. The pencil should stay in the groove and make a nice line that is on the grain of your backing. This groove is between two foundation warp and weft threads. Warp threads run lengthwise and weft threads run crosswise.

I find this task easier to handle if I turn the backing to do each side. I like to hold the pencil in front of me, grasp the backing just behind the pencil, and pull straight away from me. Since I have short arms, I sometimes have to repeat this process a couple of times depending on the size of the pattern.

Draw along the straight of grain with a carpenter's pencil.

If the pattern has multiple borders or an inside border line, use this technique to make sure your borders are straight. Since we're hooking primitive rugs, we don't need to be perfect anyplace else. Go over any pencil lines with a black marker and make sure the label on your marker says it is permanent ink. You don't want to use anything that could bleed through your rug if it should get wet.

Once you establish your straight-grain edges, you're ready to draw your design on your chosen backing. Many of the rug design patterns in this book will need to be enlarged. The patterns are either given at 100% or drawn to scale on a grid but reduced in size. You can use the grid as a guide for enlarging the pattern by hand, or take the pattern to a copy shop and ask them to enlarge it by the percentage indicated on the pattern. From your full-size pattern, make templates using heavy paper, lightweight cardboard, manila folders, or template plastic. Trace around the templates onto your backing as directed in the project instructions. Go over any pencil lines with a permanent black marker. These are primitive designs, so you don't need to worry about perfection when it comes to placement. Any slight variations help make the rug uniquely yours.

With the outer edges established and the pattern drawn, you need to put a couple stay-stitching rows about 3/4" to 1" from the outside edge of your pattern. I recommend a couple rows of zigzag stitches. If you don't have a sewing machine, a couple of rows of a running stitch will work. Stitch the rows right next to each other or one on top of the other. Stay stitch the corners on a diagonal as shown. Eventually you will cut just outside this line, and this will prevent the backing from raveling while you are finishing the edges of your rug.

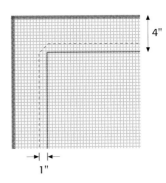

Hooking a Rug

The following instructions assume that you are right-handed. If you are left-handed, reverse the directions and hold the wool in your right hand and the hook in your left hand.

If this is your very first attempt at rug hooking, practice with some extra backing and wool strips. Start hooking in a straight line at the furthest point from you on the backing and then down toward you. Most people find that this is the easiest way for them to hook a rug. Eventually you'll learn how to hook in all directions. You should also determine how you like to hold your hook. Many people hold the hook like a pencil, while others hold it in the palm of their hand. Try both ways to see which is more natural and comfortable for you.

The following are the basic steps for rug hooking:

1. Place your backing on your frame or in your hoop, centering the area you will begin to hook first. If you have a frame with gripper strips, simply place the backing over the grippers and make sure it is taut. You want the backing taut but not skin tight. With a quilting hoop, position the backing over the smaller hoop, place the larger hoop on top, and tighten the bolt. To avoid permanent crease marks or flattened wool loops, do not leave your project in the quilting hoop overnight or for extended periods of time.

2. Pick up the first strip in your left hand. Holding the strip between your thumb and forefinger, place your left hand underneath your backing.

3. With the hook in your right hand, push the end of the hook through an opening on the top of the backing. Place the wool strip in the curve of the hook and pull the end up through the hole so that about ½" shows. This will be just the tail end of the strip.

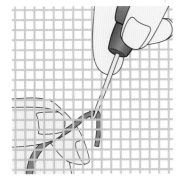

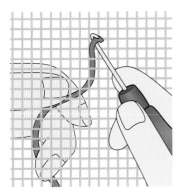

4. Place your hook into the very next hole and pull up your first real loop. Use your hand underneath the backing to help guide the strip onto the hook and pull the loop

through the hole. Loops should be as high as the strip is wide. For #8 strips used in this book, pull the loops up ¼". When the loop is the right height, gently slide the hook out.

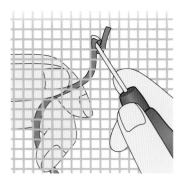

5. Insert the hook into every second or third hole. Which hole you use will depend on the thickness of your wool. The loops should touch each other but not be crammed together.

6. Continue in this manner until you are near the end of your strip of wool. Don't panic. Just pull the end of the strip up through the hole. All strips begin and end on the topside. There should be no ends sticking out on the backside.

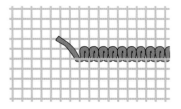

7. Insert the hook back into the hole where the previous strip ended. Pull up the end of the next strip into that same hole. There will always be either a loop or two tails in a hole of the backing. Stagger the starting and stopping points from row to row. You don't want tails to line up.

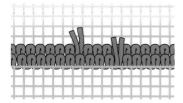

8. Occasionally grasp the tails and clip them off to the height of the loops surrounding them.

9. Remember to always hook inside the black line of your pattern.

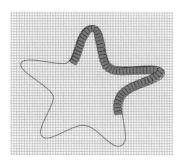

Dragging strips from one spot to another on the backside of the backing is a no-no. Always stop and start your strip of wool even if it's only a couple of holes away from where you want to use the color again. In other words, cut off your strip rather than skip holes to hook a short distance away. You do not want crossovers, twists, bumps, or lumps on the backside of your rug. The backside should be as pretty as the topside but flat. A smooth rug on the back gives years of even wear.

Rug Hooking in a Nutshell

Before you pull that first loop, keep these things in mind:

- Each loop should be as high as your strip is wide.
- Insert the hook into every second or third hole. The loops should touch each other, and no backing should show.
- Start and end a strip in the same hole.
- Stagger the starting and stopping points from row to row.
- Don't start or stop in a corner.
- Don't drag your strips from one spot to another on the underside of your rug.
- Don't twist your strips.
- Hook inside the drawn black pattern lines.
- Start hooking in the center of the rug and work toward the outside.

Hooking the Designs

When you feel comfortable with the basics of pulling up loops, start hooking your rug. Outline the motif in the centermost part of your rug. Hook just to the inside of the drawn black lines, not on them. Then fill the area in. Look closely at the photograph of the rug to get an idea of the flow to hooking each motif.

For example, the basket in Primitive Posies was hooked horizontally so it looks like a woven basket. The rows of loops in the horse of Tally Ho show muscle and movement. How you hook the motifs is entirely up to you, but following the contour is usually a good guideline. After you finish filling in each motif, go around the outside of it with one row of background loops. This locks in the contour of the motif and gives you an idea of how the background will look.

Hooking the Background

Hooking backgrounds can be boring, but there are a couple of ways to make them more interesting. First hook two rows around the motifs and at least one row around the outer edge. Then you can hook in a meandering fashion or hook in specific directions.

Meandering

To meander, take a permanent-ink marker and draw a light wandering line through the background. Hook on the line and use it as a guide for filling in the background.

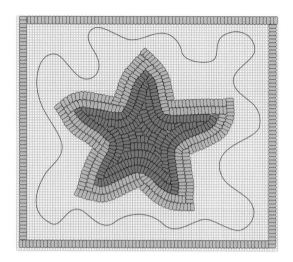

Directional Hooking

Directional hooking was seen in many of the early primitive rugs. It makes me wonder if that was the way the frame was positioned and the rug hooker was only comfortable hooking in one direction. Whatever the reason, you can use directional hooking to make backgrounds more interesting. See the illustration below for some ideas.

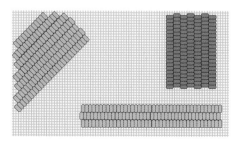

Hooking Corners

Although hooking corners isn't hard, corners are not a good place to stop or start a new strip of wool. To avoid this, start and end a strip a few loops before the corner. Hook toward you along the edge. When you come to the corner, turn your frame so that you continue to hook toward you. Use your frame in ways that will make things easier for you.

Hooking Circles

Circles are easy if you start from the outside and work in. Outline and fill is the rule of thumb with circles. Here is one place, however, where you will most likely end up with one single tail in a hole. That will be in the very center of the circle and it should present no problem.

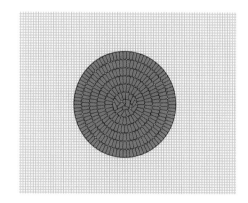

Hooking with Wool Yarn and Cotton

The same principle of pulling up one loop at a time goes whether you're hooking with wool strips, bulky wool yarn, or cotton homespun fabric strips.

Bulky wool yarn is fun to work with. The lanolin in the undyed, natural wool yarn makes your hands feel good. With wool yarn I recommend cutting lengths no longer than 24". As you pull each loop, twist the yarn strand underneath. This keeps the wool yarn from pulling apart or being split by your hook. The cat and tree trunk in Old Homestead (page 81 and below right)

were hooked with bulky, natural wool yarn in dark brown. Wool yarn was also used in Floyd (page 66 and below left) and Tally Ho (page 70 and bottom of this page).

When hooking with cotton, tear your strips. Tear the strips about $3/4$" wide, pull off any excess strings, and start to hook by folding the beginning end of the strip in half lengthwise. Folding makes it easier to pull up the strip. Don't worry about keeping the cotton strip folded as you continue to hook. With homespun cotton, both sides are the same and the way the extra-wide strip feeds naturally adds a character and charm you can't achieve with $1/4$"-wide wool strips.

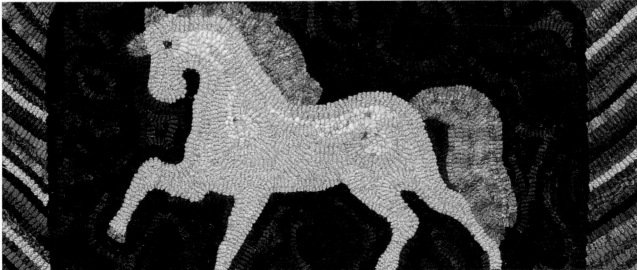

FINISHING YOUR RUG

Once you complete the hooking on your project, you need to finish the edges of your rug with binding tape or by whipping with yarn. Choose one of these methods and follow the instructions below. Then steam your finished project as directed on page 37.

Binding

The easiest and simplest method of binding your edges is to use 1¼" binding tape. Binding tape, available at rug-hooking specialty shops and through mail-order sources, comes in many different colors. Try to match the color of the binding tape to the last row of hooking. If you can't match the color exactly, choose the color that is closest.

To determine the amount of binding tape you'll need, measure the outside perimeter of your rug. Add 12" to the perimeter measurement to allow for shrinkage. Wash the binding tape before applying it to the rug, as some colors bleed.

I sew the binding tape on before I begin hooking. This makes it easier to hook right up to the binding tape and you end up with a nice finished edge when you turn back the binding. Place the tape on the outer-edge line of the pattern, right side facing the design. Sew by hand or machine, stitching as close to the edge as possi-

ble (no more than ⅛" seam). Use a small running stitch if sewing by hand. Ease the tape around the corner. You can also sew one strip of binding tape to each side of the rug. If you do this, be sure to leave at least 1" extra at the ends of each strip.

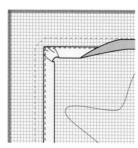

Hook the outside row as close as possible to the binding tape. When the hooking is complete, cut away the backing just beyond the stay stitching. Fold the binding back, miter the corners, and sew the binding tape to the back of the rug with heavy-duty thread.

Hooker's Hint
You can use T-pins to hold the binding out of the way when hooking the outermost rows.

Hooker's Hint

If you want to hang your rug on the wall, there are two ways to hang it. One way is to sew a sleeve on the backside and slide a rod through it. Another way requires the use of a carpet tack strip. Cut the tack strip to the width of the rug and nail it to the wall with the tacks facing up. Then press your rug onto the strip and voilà!

Whipping

The term *whipping* means to wrap cording or the folded edge of the backing with wool yarn using a whip stitch. There are two ways to whip the edges of a rug. One way is with a piece of cording and the other is without.

To whip a rug, you need three-ply wool yarn in a color that matches or coordinates with the outer edge of your rug. Paternayan-brand three-ply wool comes in many colors and can be purchased at most needlepoint stores. A three-ply piece of yarn that measures two yards long will cover 2" to 3". Whatever the perimeter of your rug is, figure that you will need that many yards of yarn. In the project materials lists, I've added an extra yard for safety. Needlepoint shops usually cut the yarn into specific lengths, so you can buy as much or as little as you need of a particular color. You'll also need a tapestry needle with a large eye. If you choose to add cording, purchase enough ¼" or ⅜" cotton cording to go around your rug. Cotton cording is available at most fabric stores. Finally, make sure to trim the backing up to the stay-stitching line before whipping the edges.

Whipping with cording: Lay a piece of ¼" or ⅜" cotton cording on the top side of the rug next to the last row of hooking. Fold the backing over and under the cording. Pin it in place. Thread the tapestry needle with a piece of yarn and whip from top to bottom and right to left, working from the topside of the rug. Keep the whipping snug but not too tight. You do not need to knot the ends of the yarn. Bury the ends in the whipping yarn as you go.

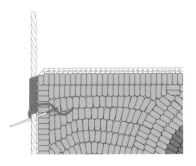

Hooker's Hint

If you have a hit-or-miss border (a multicolor border that uses all the colors in the rug) and want to whip the edges of your rug, buy three-ply yarn in several colors that appear in the border. Untwist the yarn and make your own three-ply yarn with the various colors. This gives the rug a nice edge that flatters the hit-or-miss borders.

Hooker's Hint

Whip the yarn so that it completely covers the backing and cording, but don't overlap the yarn. That will make the edges too bulky and they won't lie flat.

Whipping without cording: Fold the backing over twice toward the top of the rug. Whip this with the yarn. Again, keep the whipping snug but not too tight.

Steaming

There is one last step before your rug is really finished. Steaming is very important and you'll be amazed at what it can do to your rug. Steaming a rug is like steaming a wrinkled suit! It makes it neat and tidy. If you hook on monk's cloth and even linen, it tends to curl, and steaming flattens it. Steaming also makes the loops look prettier and more uniform. Steaming is the final touch that makes the rug lie flat and look finished.

The projects in this book are small enough that you can use your ironing board for this final process, so set it up and plug in your iron. You don't need a steam iron, but you want to set the iron on the hottest setting.

Use an old terry-cloth dishtowel. Wet it thoroughly and ring it out. With your rug topside down, put the towel on the rug. With your iron, press but do not move the iron around. I like to put the iron down, hold it in place until steam rises, about 8 to 12 seconds, and then move it to the next spot. This process is slow but it makes a big difference in the look of the finished rug. Rewet the towel as needed and continue to press the backside of the rug. Turn your rug over and repeat the process on the topside. When you have completely steamed both the topside and backside of your rug, find a place to lay it flat. Now leave it there for 24 hours and let it dry.

Be Kind to Your Rug

Don't use the beater bars on a vacuum to clean a hooked rug. They can suck out the strips. Use the upholstery attachment. And do not shake a hooked rug; vigorous handling of the backing may cause some of the loops to come out.

Simple Ways to Dye Wool and Get Primitive Colors

"Aha, the mad chemist is at work!" That's what my husband has been known to say when he comes home from work to find white enamel pots in the laundry-room sink, wet wool hanging on a drying rack, and fluffed, folded colorful wool just out of the dryer. Dyeing is fun for me; I call it playtime, but it's not for everyone.

We wouldn't even need to dye wool if we could walk into a store and buy exactly what we want. Unfortunately, I haven't found that store yet. Trust me; I have looked. But the variety of wool available now is far superior to what it was just a few years ago. Solid-colored wool was plentiful then, but good textured wool selections were limited. Due to the increased popularity of primitive rug hooking and demanding consumers, we now have an abundance of wonderful textured wool to choose from. Even all these options don't guarantee that we'll find the exact colored wool we want. There are, however, three ways you can get the colors you want:

1. The Easiest Way. Buy hand-dyed wool from someone who specializes in dyeing wool and produces colors you like. This is simple and easy, but you'll pay a premium for their time and expertise.

2. The Fun and Challenging Way. Dye your own wool. Jump in, make mistakes, and play. You can't imagine the satisfaction you'll get when you've dyed the exact color you had in mind.

3. The Scavenger Hunt. Try to find perfect colors by visiting thrift stores, friends' closets, or wool stores. Some love the hunt, but it can be like looking for a needle in a haystack, and it takes away valuable rug-hooking time.

Three Factors That Affect Dyeing Results

If you choose the fun and challenging route, there are three things that will vary regardless of how closely you follow directions. The most significant one is water. The other two are the original color of the wool and the dye you use. If you keep this in mind, you won't panic or be disappointed when you follow a dye formula to the letter and you don't get the same color someone else does.

Water is the biggest factor that affects dyeing, and I could write a whole chapter on this subject. Since I started dyeing wool for my rugs, I have lived in five states. I had always heard water caused some variation, but the results of my dyeing efforts proved that. At one point I did some in-depth research and conducted a controlled experiment. I enlisted the help of dyers in four other states; we used the same fabrics, the same dye formulas, and the same dyeing process—but different water. The results were amazing. There was a great deal of variation in our end products, with blue varying the most, followed by green. I've found that even water in your own home can vary in mineral content and acidity from day to day, depending on rainfall, water levels, and chlorine content. The original source of the water will also influence the water chemistry, as will the pipes in your home. There's really not much you can do to control water. Simply be aware that it can affect your results from one time to the next. Dye more fabric than you think you'll need each time you dye if you are concerned about having consistency of color for a specific project.

Equipment for Dyeing

Here's a run-down of the basic equipment you'll need for dyeing. Depending on the type of dyeing you plan to do, some items may be optional.

- Dye pots, preferably white enameled pots, 12-quart size or larger
- 2-cup heatproof measuring cup
- Noniodized or kosher salt
- White vinegar
- Measuring spoons
- Dye spoons
- Stirring spoons or long-handled tongs
- Notebook to keep records
- Apron, latex gloves, heavy rubber gloves, and a dust mask for maximum protection

Supplies for Dyeing Wools

Hooker's Hint

When looking at color and planning colors for your rug, use natural light if at all possible. Fluorescent lighting changes colors drastically. Use a full-spectrum bulb or lamp when you must use artificial lighting.

Once equipment has been set aside for dyeing, do not use it for food again because it would be unsafe. A white enamel pot is best for dyeing, because it allows you to see the color of the dye. If you can only find or afford one pot to start out with, get a 12-quart pot. Two pots are better, and if at all possible get pots that will hold between 12 and 16 quarts. Aluminum pots and pans are not recommended, because vinegar and kosher salt, which are used in the dyeing process, can cause them to pit. Pitting can cause pans to leach chemicals into the dye bath and create colors you don't want.

Dye spoons range from $1/2$ teaspoon to $1/128$ teaspoon. They can be purchased from most of the suppliers listed on page 95.

Grocery-Store Dyes

Your favorite grocery store is a wonderful source for dye materials. Let's start in the produce section. Did you know that onion skins can produce a soft golden tone in a natural colored wool? Beets are another good dye source if you're looking for a muted light red to a pale purple.

Move over a couple of aisles and you'll find coffee and tea. If you're not a tea drinker, you'll be surprised to see the wide variety of flavored teas available. Cranberry-apple tea produces some wonderful shades of pink depending on the number of tea bags you use and the original color of the wool. The samples shown (before and after) were dyed using six tea bags of cranberry-apple tea in a pot of water.

Before-and-After Samples of Wool Dyed with Cranberry-Apple Tea

Don't forget that most grocery stores carry Rit Dye in both powder and liquid form. Remember, if it stains your hands, counters, or clothes, it has possibilities. How about Kool-Aid? I bet you'll look at items in the grocery store differently from now on.

First Step for All Dyeing

Wet all wool before it is dyed. Wetting the wool opens the wool fibers, thus allowing the dye solution to soak through the wool completely. Place the wool you wish to dye in a one- to three-gallon pot or plastic pail that is filled with hot water and a small amount of liquid detergent. Ivory liquid dishwashing soap is perfect. A half teaspoon of liquid soap to a pot is more than enough. Let it soak at least 30 minutes but preferably overnight.

There are also commercial wetting agents (such as Synthrapol and Wetter Than Wet) that allow you to soak the wool for only 20 minutes, but most of you have dishwashing liquid already under the sink. By the time you gather the rest of your equipment, the half hour will have passed and your wool will be ready for dyeing.

Hooker's Hint

Wool appears darker in color when it is wet than when it is dry.

Onion-Skin Dyeing

Onion-skin dyeing has been going on for years, and there are a couple of different methods you can choose to make your dye solution. You can dye up to $1/2$ yard of wool following these instructions. Make the dye solution using one of the two methods.

Option 1: Pack a two-quart pot with onion skins and add six cups of hot water. Simmer on low heat for about 20 minutes. Remove the onion skins and use the solution that remains in the pot to dye your wool. Transfer the solution to a larger pot (12 quarts) and continue as instructed below.

Option 2: If you want to avoid the mess of removing wet onion skins from your dye pot, stuff the leg of a pair of panty hose with dry onion skins and put that in a 12-quart white enamel pot with six cups of water; then simmer. Make sure the panty hose is a light color and has been washed. You don't want the panty hose color to bleed into your dye solution. Simmer the onion skins 20 to 30 minutes and then remove them.

Now that you have a pot of onion-skin dye solution, add enough water until the pot is two-thirds full. Heat the pot on medium high until the water is steaming. Add your wet wool to the pot. Push it down with tongs or a long-handled spoon. Reduce the heat to medium and continue to cook for approximately 20 minutes, stirring occasionally. If you like the color you see after 20 minutes, pour $1/4$ to $1/3$ cup of vinegar into the pot to set the color. If you want it darker, let it simmer 10 more minutes before adding the vinegar. Continue to cook the wool for 20 minutes but do not let it boil. Now turn off the heat and let it cool.

Be Patient—Let It Cool

Letting the wool cool in the pot is very important. There are a couple of reasons. While the wool cools it continues to soak up any residual dye in the pot. If you were in a hurry, dumped out the wool and wetted it with cold water, you could ruin your beautiful dye job. Cold water on hot wool causes it to felt or get too thick for rug hooking. If you are in a hurry, dump the wool into a sink and let the water drain off. The wool will cool faster now that it's out of the hot water, but be patient and let it cool until it's easy to touch.

Coffee and Tea Dyeing

Both coffee and tea produce a dye solution that you can use to obtain a mellow yellow or camel color when dyeing over an off-white wool. If you have wool that is too bright, a quick dip into either of these solutions will dull it.

To dye with coffee, put four tablespoons of instant coffee into two cups of boiling water; then pour that into a dye pot half full of water. Add ¼ to ½ yard of off-white or pale oatmeal-colored wool. Once you achieve the color you want, add some vinegar and continue to cook about 20 more minutes to set the color. Let it cool; rinse your wool with fresh water, and dry. Coffee dyeing will produce a camel-colored wool that can be used as is or overdyed again with a commercial dye. By varying the amount of coffee and wool, you can produce several shades of camel-colored wool.

To dye with tea, start with four tea bags and simmer them in about 4" of water in a 12-quart pot. Remove the tea bags and add a few small pieces (3" x 12" strips) of off-white wool and simmer 10 to 20 minutes. The longer you simmer, the darker the color. Different-flavored teas will produce different colors. You have to be willing to experiment and play the dyeing game! Add vinegar to set the color, simmer another 20 minutes, let cool, rinse, and dry.

Hooker's Hint

Color changes can happen quickly with both tea and coffee, so watch what is happening. Only you know what color you are looking for, so start with less. You can always add more to make it darker, but you can't take it away once you've made the wool too dark.

Before-and-After Samples of Wool Dyed with Coffee

Stewing and Marrying

Stewing and marrying are two types of dyeing techniques that are often done without any added dyes. Both techniques involve cooking wools together to achieve more uniformity in color. With marrying, you use similar-colored wools; stewing involves wools in different colors.

Marrying

Imagine that you have several pieces of red wool. One is an orange-red plaid, another is a cranberry herringbone, and the third is a crayon-red check. You'd like to use them all in your rug, but they don't really go together. By marrying these similar pieces of red wool, you can use them together. The following steps describe the process:

1. Wet the wool prior to starting the pot as directed in "First Step for All Dyeing" on page 41.
2. Put a tablespoon of Arm & Hammer washing soda or a detergent that does not contain bleach in a large enamel pot of water. Bring the water temperature up to medium high.
3. After the detergent has dissolved, add your wet wool. The various pieces of red wool will bleed, giving you a wonderful pot full of red-colored water.
4. Simmer on medium heat for 15 to 20 minutes, and then add ¼ to ⅓ cup of vinegar.
5. Continue to simmer for another 15 to 20 minutes or until the water has cleared. Let the wool cool in the pot.

6. Rinse the wool, dry it, and marvel at the beautiful pieces of wool that now work perfectly together.

What if you want light, medium, and dark shades of a color? Start by putting the darkest colored wool into the pot. When you have nice, dark water, add your vinegar. Let some of the color get soaked up into the wool already in the pot. When the water is about half as dark as it was, put a medium shade of wool into the pot and let it soak up some of the color. Do this again when the water is lighter still with a lighter shade of wool. Now let it all simmer for about 15 minutes. Once the wool is cooled, rinsed, and dried, you should have a light, medium, and dark shade of the original dark color.

Stewing

Stewing works very much the same way as marrying, but you use different-colored wools. Maybe you have some lime greens, medium greens, and teal blues that you'd like to use for grass or as a background. Or you have a bright, garish yellow and a small piece of purple, but you'd really like a nice, calm, dull yellow. Perhaps you have pieces of blue, red, brown, green, purple, orange, and black, and you want a dirty-looking, antique background color. Stewing these combinations in a pot using the marrying procedure will produce some wonderful, usable wool.

The trick with stewing is to get a color wheel first and look at it. We all know red and yellow make orange, but did you know a little blue added to a pot of bright orange will dull the orange down to a subdued color just right for a primitive rug? Colors opposite each other on the color wheel are called complements. If you add a little of a color's complement to the dye solution, you will dull down the color. But be careful; a little goes a long way. Add too much of a complement and you make mud.

Commercial Dyes

Commercial dyes are used to overdye wool to produce a specific color. For example, by using specific guidelines and formulas, you can put camel-colored wool into a dye bath made up of small quantities of a specific dry red dye and water, and you'll end up with a rich, rusty red wool. You can overdye any wool that is too bright or garish and get wonderful, primitive colors that will be perfect for your projects.

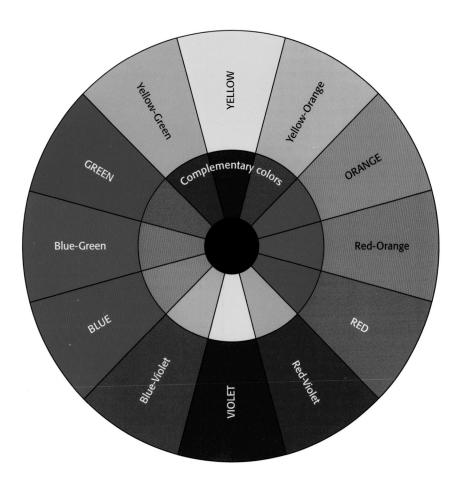

Remember that dyeing is fun and there are endless possibilities. It is not for those who don't like to play with color. You have to accept the fact that you'll make lots of mistakes before you are in control of what goes into the pot and what comes out. If I asked three people for oatmeal- or camel-colored wool, we'd have three different shades of oatmeal- or camel-colored wool. We all see color differently, and red to one person is cranberry or cherry to another. This doesn't seem like much, but it can produce different dyeing results.

As I mentioned earlier, water, the color of your wool, and the fact that dyes can vary from packet to packet often cause a specific dye formula to produce different colors. Fortunately we are looking for primitive colors, and the old rugs were not exactly perfect. All of the variables I have mentioned work in favor of the primitive rug hooker.

With commercial dyes, there are many great colors you can achieve without complicated formulas. Two commercial dye brands that I use regularly are Cushing and ProChem, but there are several others that produce fabulous colors. Start by using a ¼ teaspoon of dye to a cup of boiling water. You can always add more dye or other colors. If you want a dirty, dull green color, I recommend trying Cushing Khaki. For a dirty, rusty red, try ProChem #255. For an antique black color, combine Cushing Olive Green, Dark Brown, and Black.

To help you get started, I've included the following steps for dyeing khaki and antique black wool.

Khaki Wool (Dirty, Dull Green)

1. Presoak ½ yard of oatmeal-, tan-, beige-, and/or taupe-colored wool. Fill a dye pot about two-thirds full of hot tap water and add a heaping tablespoon of non-iodized salt. Put the pot on the stove and turn the heat to medium high.
2. Dissolve ¼ teaspoon of Cushing Khaki dye (use dye spoons) in one cup of boiling water.
3. Add the cup of dye solution to a pot of water that is close to boiling.
4. Add your presoaked wool. Lower the heat to medium and simmer for 20 minutes.
5. Add ¼ to ⅓ cup of vinegar and simmer 20 more minutes. Turn off the heat and let the wool cool.

Before-and-After Samples of Wool Colored with Khaki Dye

Hooker's Hint

Some dyes come in plastic, resealable bags. Mark the dye color on the resealable bag inside the dye envelope. Dry dye doesn't always look like what's printed on the envelope, and it can be easy to mix them up.

Antique Black Wool

You will need Cushing dyes in Olive Green, Dark Brown, and Black. Gather up ½ yard of wool. Any color will do. Try purple, red, brown, Kelly green, chartreuse, gray, and even orange wool.

1. Presoak all the wool.
2. Fill a dye pot about two-thirds full of hot tap water and add a heaping tablespoon of non-iodized salt. Put the pot on the stove and turn the heat to medium high.
3. Measure the following amounts of dye with dye spoons, not measuring spoons, and place into a heat-resistant measuring cup:

    1 teaspoon Cushing Olive Green

    ½ teaspoon Cushing Dark Brown

    ¼ teaspoon Cushing Black
4. Pour a cup of boiling water into the measuring cup and stir thoroughly. Pour the entire cup into the dye pot.
5. Slowly add your wool to the pot. Let it cook for 20 minutes. Stir occasionally and watch that it doesn't boil.
6. Add ¼ to ⅓ cup of white vinegar, stir, and continue to cook for another 20 minutes. The water will become clear while it cooks. Turn off the heat and let the wool cool.

Words of Encouragement

Dyeing is fun and you can use almost anything to try and change the color of wool. Remember, back in the early days of rug hooking, berries, flowers, nuts, and bark were all used to produce colors for dyeing. Don't be afraid to try. Just remember to relax, pick a time when you won't be interrupted, keep good written records of what you do, and don't worry. Playing in the dye pots is like playing in the sandbox. Enjoy and have fun. There are a couple of very good dye books written specifically for dyeing primitive colors. See "Resources" on page 94 for the books I recommend.

Hooker's Hint

Dye more fabric than you need. Having a little extra is better than running out.

PRIMITIVE RUG PROJECTS

At this point, you have either read the previous sections of the book or skipped right to the good stuff. For those of you who skipped ahead, I understand. But if you're fairly new to rug hooking, I do suggest that you go back and read what you've missed. Reading about the tools and techniques will help you avoid problems.

I hooked all of these rugs using a #8 cut, or ¼"-wide strips. The materials lists assume the use of that cut. When several different colors of wool are listed for one area of the rug, the quantity is given as total yardage. Calculating yardage requirements for rug hooking is not an exact science. New wool off the bolt usually measures 58" to 60" wide. After washing and drying, the wool shrinks down to 54" wide. I use that width to estimate yardages, and I've given ranges of yardage needed. If you are new to rug hooking, plan on using the higher amount. As you gain experience, you will become more efficient and will be able to use more of each strip. I usually tell students to fold their wool in four generous layers over the area they want to fill. That works out to be four-plus times the size of the area to be covered; beginners may want to use five times the area to be covered. It's best to plan on the heavy side.

There are no rules that say you have to hook these rugs exactly as I did. For each project, I've listed the materials required to make the rug as shown in the photograph. I've also included a section called "Hints on Fabric Selection" to give

Hooker's Hint

I am very nearsighted and I use that to my advantage. I take my glasses off and look at the colors; I can easily tell if something pops out or if a part of the rug blends into another area too much, muddying the design. Your goal for a primitive look is to use subtle colors but still show contrast between them.

you some other options. Whatever colors you choose, I suggest that you lay them out on the floor, step back, and see how they look together. If a color pops out at you, it's probably not a good idea to use it. When I say "pop," I mean it is too bright, too garish, or your eye immediately goes to it. You want the rug to be pleasing with no one area that jumps out at you.

If this is your very first hooked rug, I suggest you start with one of the beginner rugs. I've organized the projects in order from easiest to more difficult, although none of them are really difficult or extremely detailed. Try something manageable that you'll be able to finish. Then move on to something a little larger and more challenging. Happy rug hooking!

General Directions for Each Project

1. Prepare your foundation following the directions on page 27.
2. Draw the outline for the pattern following the directions for each rug and referring to "Drawing the Pattern" on pages 27–29.
3. Use a permanent marker to draw around each template and retrace the border lines drawn in pencil.
4. Give some thought to the binding technique you want to use to finish the rug. If you want to use binding tape, remember to sew it on before you hook to the edge of the pattern.
5. Cut your wool strips on the straight of grain from pieces that are about 18" long and 3" wide. Cut small quantities at one time.

TWO LITTLE STARS

 This simple little beginner project is easy and fun to do. The color possibilities are endless. This project can become a table mat, pillow, or the cover of a small bench. I have never had a beginner student not finish this project. If you want to make your project into a pillow, like the one shown here, see the instructions for Two Little Stars Pillow on page 52.

Materials

Yardages are generously estimated and based on 54"-wide wool fabric.

- Backing, 22" x 17" (26" x 21" if using a hoop)
- ¼ yard *total* of gold wool for stars and border
- ¼ yard *total* of red wool for background and border
- 8" x 18" piece of green wool for border
- 46 yards of green 3-ply wool yarn for whipping OR 1⅝ yards of green binding tape

Drawing the Pattern

1. On the piece of backing, draw a 14" x 9" rectangle for the outer edge of the rug.
2. Draw the inside border so that it measures 11" x 6".
3. Make a template from the star pattern on page 53. Position the star template inside the 11" x 6" rectangle and trace around it to make two stars.

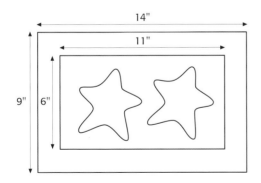

Finished Size: 14" x 9"

Hints on Fabric Selection

- Take the opportunity to choose three of your favorite colors for stars, background, and border.
- Use several small pieces of golds and reds (or colors of your choice) to make up the ¼ yard needed for the stars and background. This will give the design more depth and interest. This is a good time to try marrying your colors together so they blend nicely. (Refer to "Marrying" on page 44.)

Hooking Order

If you are going to use binding tape to finish this project, add it now or after step 2. See "Binding" on page 35.

1. Hook the stars.
2. Hook the background around the stars in the 11" x 6" rectangle. Outline the area first and then fill it in, echoing the star shapes.
3. Hook the inner row of gold all the way around, followed by one row of red, one row of gold, and three rows of green.
4. Finish the rug according to the directions in "Finishing Your Rug" on page 35. Most of my students finish this project with binding tape.

Two Little Stars Pillow

To make your hooked piece into a pillow, you will follow the basic instructions for the rug. Before you begin rug hooking, however, you must cut wool border fabric and follow steps 1–3 under "Assembly" at right.

Additional Materials

- 3/4 yard of coordinating wool, cotton homespun, or brushed cotton for borders and pillow back
- 10" x 16" pillow form

Cutting

From the border and pillow backing fabric, cut:
2 pieces, 2½" x 10"
2 pieces, 2½" x 18"
1 piece, 8" x 19"
1 piece, 9" x 19"

Assembly

Use ½" seam allowances throughout.

1. Complete the steps in "Drawing the Pattern" on page 51. Then position the 2½" x 10" border pieces on each side of the pattern that you've drawn onto your backing. The right sides of the border pieces should face the pattern and their edges need to extend ½" outside the drawn lines. Stitch ½" from the raw edge of the border, along the drawn line of the pattern. Press the borders away from the center.

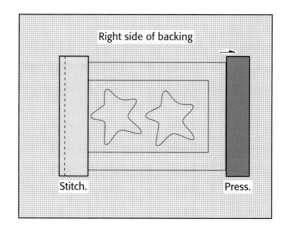

2. Sew the 2½" x 18" border pieces to the top and bottom in the same manner as the side border pieces. Make sure the right sides of the border pieces face the pattern, and align the edge of the border fabric ½" away from the edge of the pattern. Press the borders away from the center.

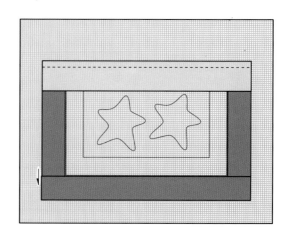

3. Refer to "Hooking Order" on page 52 and hook the pattern according to the directions. Be sure to hook right up to the edge of the pillow border fabric.

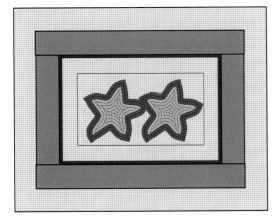

Hook to the edge.

4. Steam your finished hooked piece (page 37). When it is dry, trim the excess backing, leaving ½" all around.

5. Hem the two pillow-backing pieces along one 19" side of each, folding and pressing the long edge under ½" and topstitching it.

6. With right sides together, align the larger backing piece to the hooked pillow top. Match the raw edges and ease it to fit. The extra fabric will add some fullness to the backing for the pillow form. Pin and stitch around the three sides.

7. Repeat step 6 to sew the second backing piece to the opposite side of the hooked pillow top.

8. Turn inside out and insert your pillow form through the opening in the back. Enjoy!

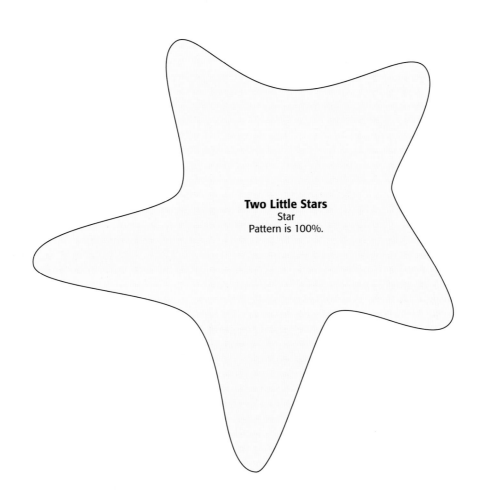

Two Little Stars
Star
Pattern is 100%.

HOUSE AND HARE

Here is another great beginner project. This one offers a few new challenges and opportunities to try hooking with wool yarn and cotton homespuns. Feel free to change the colors to make this your house and your bunny—the one who eats your pansies and other tasty green things growing in your garden.

Materials

Yardages are generously estimated and based on 54"-wide wool fabric.

- Backing, 25" x 18" (29" x 22" if using a hoop)
- ½ yard of khaki wool for the background
- 12" x 18" piece of black-and-navy plaid wool for the roof and outer border
- 8" x 18" piece of burgundy-blue-and-gray plaid wool for the house
- 8" x 18" piece of green heather, herringbone, or small check wool for the tree
- 4" x 18" piece of dark red plaid wool for the foundation and chimney
- 2" x 18" piece of beige or oatmeal wool for the windows
- 2" x 18" piece of red wool for the door
- 10 yards of dark, bulky wool yarn for the bunny and tree trunk
- 55 yards of black or navy 3-ply wool yarn for whipping OR 2 yards of black or navy binding tape

Drawing the Pattern

1. On the piece of backing, draw a 17" x 10" rectangle for the outer edge of the rug.
2. Make templates from the house, tree, and rabbit patterns on pages 56–57.
3. Position the house template so that it is about 2" in from the outside border on the left. The height of the chimney should be about 2" down from the top. Trace around the templates onto the backing.

Finished Size: 17" x 10"

Hints on Fabric Selection

- Select colors that will make the house look like your own.
- Use brown plaid or herringbone wool for the bunny and tree trunk if you don't have any bulky wool yarn.
- Substitute a taupe small plaid cotton homespun for the windows and use a red-and-black small check cotton homespun for the front door.
- Try an orange-rust-and-red plaid wool or cotton check homespun to make the tree in fall colors.
- You can change the background color; just make sure it provides enough contrast so that you can still recognize the house, tree, and rabbit.

4. Position the tree and rabbit templates so that there is room enough for at least two rows of background around each. Trace.

Hooking Order

If you are going to use simple binding tape to finish this project, add it now or after step 3. See "Binding" on page 35.

1. Start by hooking the roof, followed by the house and then the foundation.
2. Fill in the windows and door and add the chimney.
3. Hook a row of background around the house.
4. Hook the tree, the rabbit, and then the background.
5. Hook one final outside row with the black-and-navy plaid to create the outer border.
6. Finish the rug according to the directions in "Finishing Your Rug" on page 35. The rug featured here was finished with black binding tape.

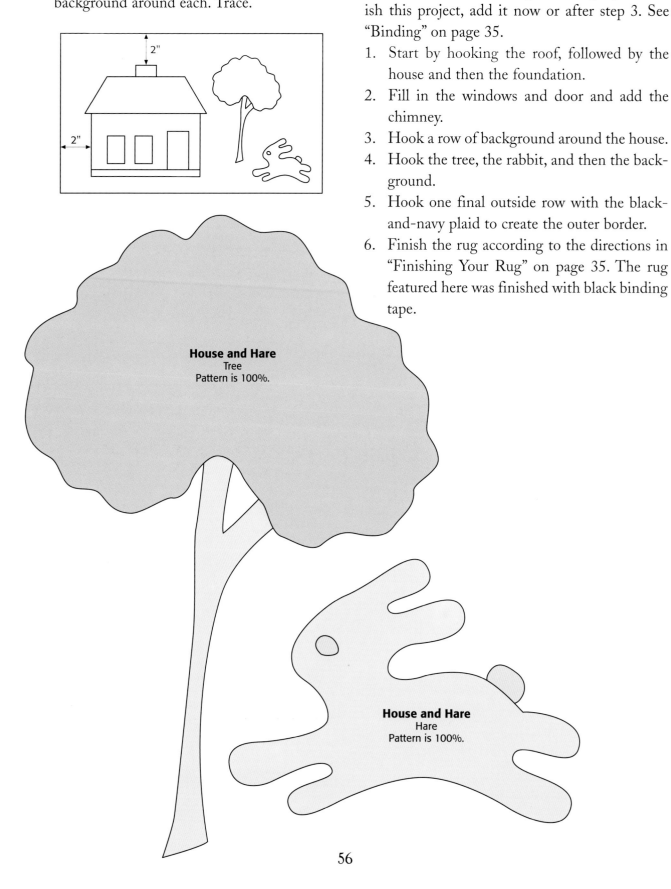

House and Hare
Tree
Pattern is 100%.

House and Hare
Hare
Pattern is 100%.

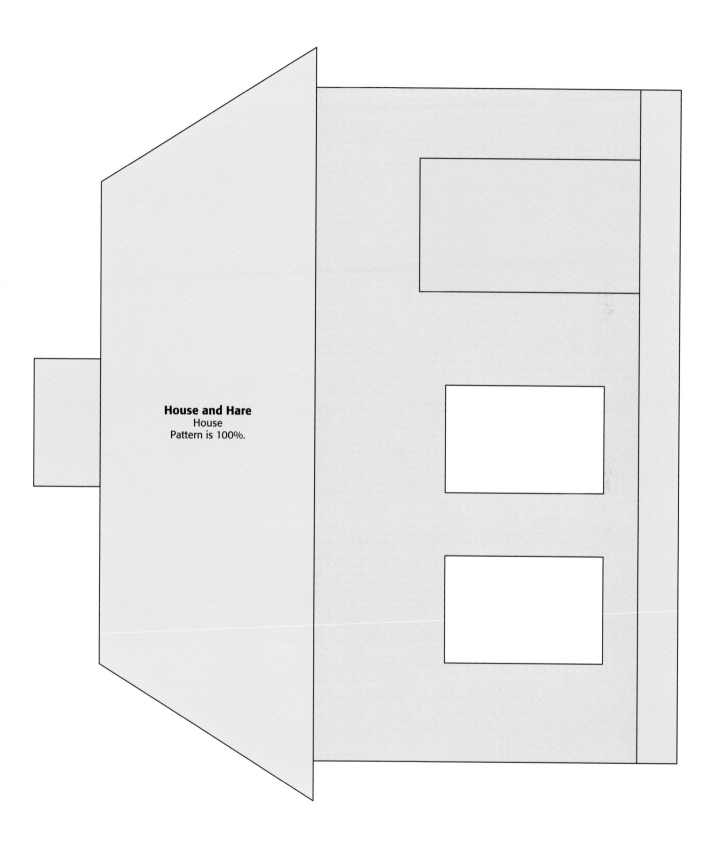

House and Hare
House
Pattern is 100%.

SWEET HEARTS

Here's a wonderful project when you want a quick gift for a friend. Leave this little mat behind after an overnight stay at the home of someone special, and you'll be welcome again any time! It makes a great chair pad, stool top, or cheery little mat on the coffee table. It's an easy beginner project and a fun place to use scraps.

Materials

Yardages are generously estimated and based on 54"-wide wool fabric.

- Backing, 22" x 19" (26" x 23" if using a hoop)
- ½ yard of black plaid wool for the background
- ⅛ to ¼ yard of red wool for hearts and wavy border
- 3" x 18" piece of bright wool to accent the hearts
- 50 yards of black 3-ply wool yarn for whipping OR 1¾ yards of binding tape

Drawing the Pattern

1. On the piece of backing, draw a 14" x 11" rectangle for the outer edge of the rug.
2. Make templates for the wavy border and the hearts from the patterns on pages 60 and 61.
3. Position the wavy template so that the corner curve is about 1" in from the corner. Trace and then flip the template to continue the wavy line.
4. Center and trace the hearts inside the wavy line.

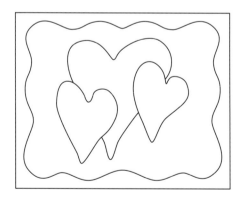

Hooking Order

If you are going to use binding tape to finish this project, add it now or after step 1. See "Binding" on page 35.

Finished Size: 14" x 11"

Hints on Fabric Selection

- For a different look, use three different colors for the hearts. Then use scraps from each heart color in the wavy outside line. This would eliminate the need for the accent lines that define the two smaller hearts.

- To add a border, hook the background behind the hearts up to the wavy line. Use a different color to hook from the wavy line out to the edge.

1. Hook the hearts first. If you choose to do them all the same color, hook one accent line on the small hearts where they overlap the large heart.
2. Hook the inside background, the wavy red border line, and the background outside the wavy border.
3. Finish the rug according to the directions in "Finishing Your Rug" on page 35. The rug featured here was finished with black binding tape.

Sweet Hearts
Hearts
Pattern is 100%.

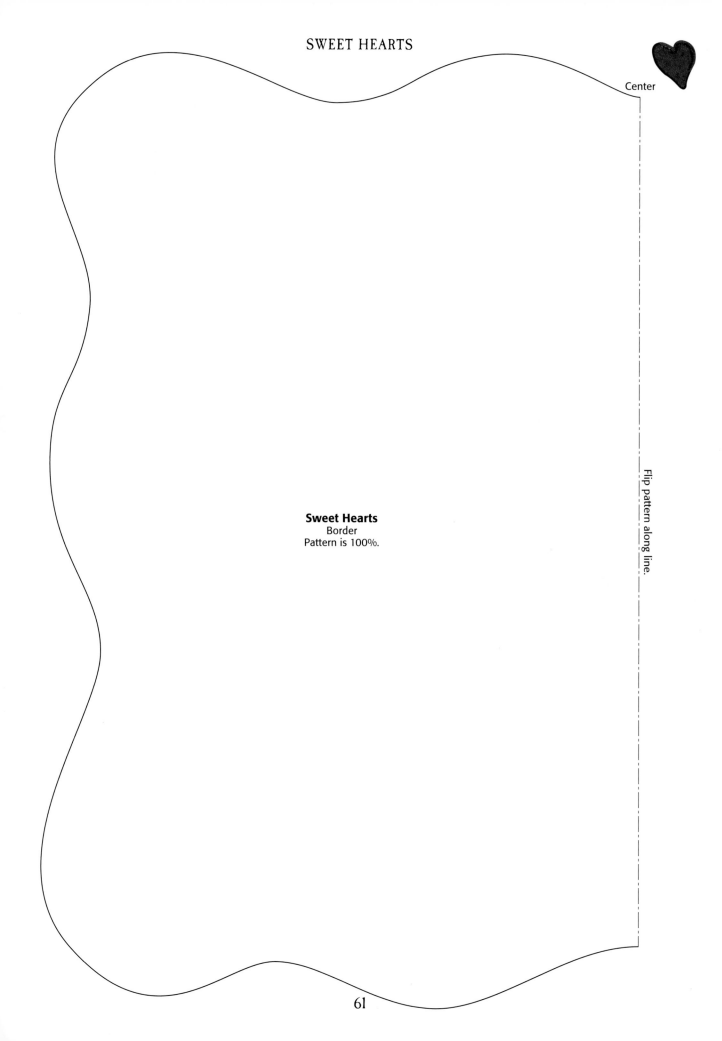

Center

Flip pattern along line.

Sweet Hearts
Border
Pattern is 100%.

PENNY CROW

This rug is an adaptation of Penny Crow Table Rug as seen in the book *Free Spirit* by Gerry Kimmel and Linda Brannock. It's done in only two colors—antique black and rusty red. I used the antique black formula given on page 47. To obtain the wonderful brick red color, use Cushing's Terra-Cotta or ProChem's Brick (255) over tan- or camel-colored wool.

Materials

Yardages are generously estimated and based on 54"-wide wool fabric.

- Backing, 34" x 26" (38" x 30" if using a hoop)
- ³/₄ to 1 yard of antique black wool for crows, pennies, star, and border
- ³/₄ to 1 yard of rusty red wool for background
- 90 yards of black 3-ply wool yarn for whipping OR 3 yards of black binding tape

Drawing the Pattern

1. On the piece of backing, draw a 26" x 18" rectangle for the outer edge of the rug.
2. Draw the inside line of the border to measure 24" x 16".
3. Make templates from the crow, star, and circle patterns on pages 64–65.
4. Position the crows in the lower third of the rug. Don't make them perfectly symmetrical. A little askew is good.
5. Place the star in the upper left.
6. Draw 17 circles around the rug in a random pattern similar to the illustration and the rug in the photograph on page 62. Use a combination of large and small circles as desired. Be sure to leave enough room so that you can get at least one row of background around each circle.

Finished Size: 26" x 18"

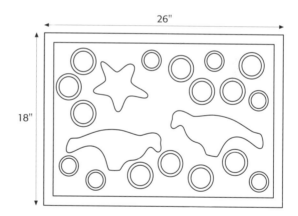

Hooking Order

If you are going to use binding tape to finish this project, add it now or after step 3. See "Binding" on page 35.

1. Hook the crows in antique black; follow up by hooking one row of background around each crow.

63

2. Hook the star and a row of background around it.

3. Hook the outside of each circle in black. Vary the number of black rows in the circles to add interest but fill each center with red.

4. Hook some of the background around the circles and then proceed to the border. The border is four rows of black. Start from the outside edge and work inward until you have four completed rows of border. Finish filling in the red background.

5. Finish the rug according to the directions in "Finishing Your Rug" on page 35. The rug featured here was finished with black binding tape.

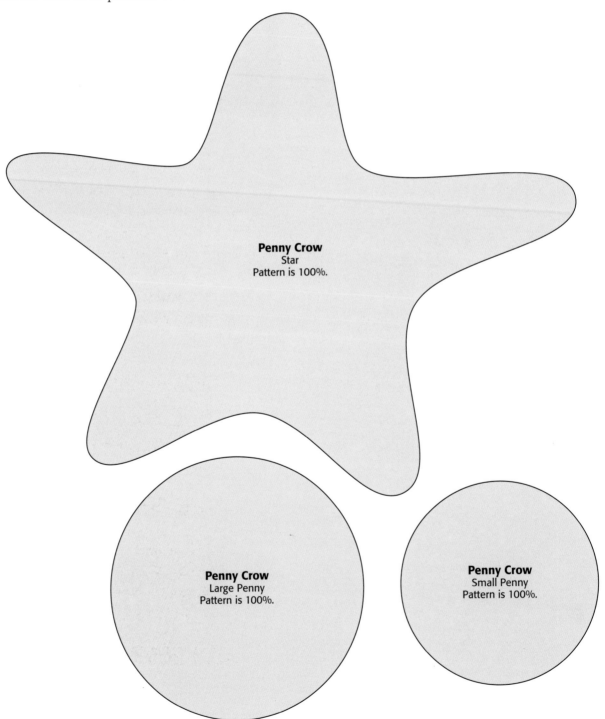

Penny Crow
Star
Pattern is 100%.

Penny Crow
Large Penny
Pattern is 100%.

Penny Crow
Small Penny
Pattern is 100%.

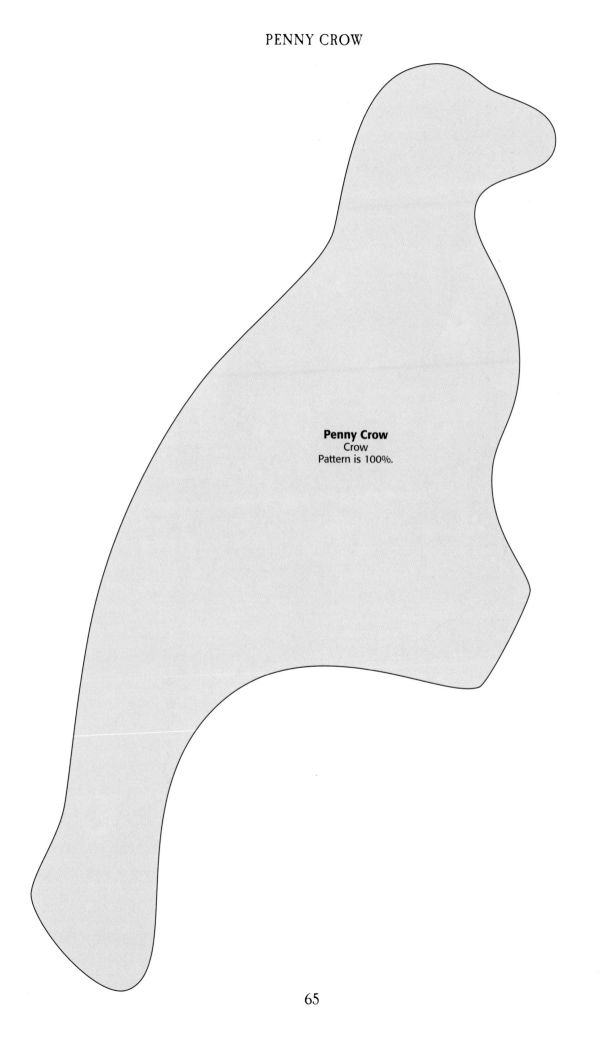

Penny Crow
Crow
Pattern is 100%.

FLOYD

Floyd is a simple little rug that is an adaptation of an antique rug I saw in someone's home. The day I started hooking this rug, I was living in South Florida, and Hurricane Floyd was heading straight toward us. Weather forecasters predicted the storm would turn away from us, but we were hunkered down in our home with galvanized-steel hurricane shutters on every window and door. When a major hurricane is staring you in the face, rug hooking is a good diversion! The hurricane did turn north at the last minute. It was then that I named this rug Floyd.

Materials

Yardages are generously estimated and based on 54"-wide wool fabric.

- Backing, 23" x 30" (27" x 34" if using a hoop)
- ¹/₂ to ³/₄ yard *total* of gray, taupe, and beige wool for cat and hit-or-miss border
- ¹/₂ to ³/₄ yard of antique black wool for background and outer border
- ¹/₂ to ³/₄ yard *total* of red, blue, green, and khaki wool for hit-or-miss border
- 3" x 18" piece *each* of red, blue, and green plaid cotton homespun fabrics for hit-or-miss border
- Scrap of rose, black, or other color wool for nose
- 1 to 3 yards of natural bulky wool yarn for cat (optional)
- 75 yards of black 3-ply wool yarn for whipping OR 2¹/₂ yards of black binding tape
- Compass (optional)

Draw Your Pattern

1. On the piece of backing, draw a 15" x 22" rectangle for the outer edge of the rug.
2. Measure in ¹/₂" and draw the inside line of the outer border. It should be 14" x 21".
3. The two opposite corners of the design are quarter circles. To draw them with a compass, set the compass to ³/₄", 1¹/₂", 2¹/₄", and 3" to draw the arc of each quarter circle. If you prefer, use the pattern on page 69 and make templates.

Finished Size: 15" x 22"

Hints on Fabric Selection

- Make sure the gray, taupe, and beige wools are compatible with each other. The bulky wool yarn should also blend nicely with these wools.
- The antique black wool can be a mixture of blacks, deep navy, and/or blue black and black green.
- An assortment of red, blue, and green wools and plaid cotton homespun fabrics make the hit-or-miss border interesting. The cotton homespun can be scraps, but make sure the pieces measure at least 12" long. You will also use antique black and the cat colors in the border.

4. The remaining two corners have squares that measure 3" x 3". Divide them in half vertically and horizontally so that each smaller square measures 1½" x 1½".

5. Enlarge the pattern 236% (page 69) for Floyd the cat, including the irregular background. Make templates with the patterns, place the background template in the center of the rug, and trace around it. Trace around the cat template inside the background.

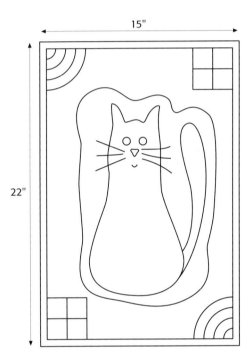

Hooking Order

If you are going to use binding tape to finish this project, add it now or after step 4. See "Binding" on page 35.

1. Outline the cat. Mix up the gray, taupe, beige, and/or natural-colored wools. Be sure to include different fabric textures, plaids, heathers, and some bulky wool yarn.

2. Hook the eyes, whiskers, and nose. Go around them once with the cat colors.

3. Finish filling in the cat.

4. Outline the cat and the outer background line behind the cat with antique black. Continue filling in the background behind the cat.

5. Hook two rows of antique black around the outer edge of the rug.

6. Hook the corners in the colors of your choice. This will depend on your wool supply.

7. Now you get to hook the fun part—the hit-or-miss border. Hit-or-miss borders have a scrappy, multicolor look and include the fabrics used in other parts of the rug. The border is hooked parallel to the outer border. Give some thought to where you place the colors. You don't want the colors grouped in areas. Make sure they are random in color, length, and starting and stopping points.

8. Finish the rug according to the directions in "Finishing Your Rug" on page 35. The rug featured here was finished with black binding tape.

Floyd
One square equals ½".
Enlarge pattern 200%, and then 118%
(236% total) to 15" x 22".

69

TALLY HO

Tally Ho is my adaptation of a rug I saw in a book on antiques. By looking closely at the tiny black-and-white picture of the rug, I saw what appeared to be a stocky workhorse. However, after living in Kentucky for many years, I decided a stately thoroughbred should take center stage on my rug. Who knows—maybe the Kentucky Derby is in his future!

Materials

Yardages are generously estimated and based on 54"-wide wool fabric.

- Backing, 35" x 25" (39" x 29" if using a hoop)
- ¾ yard of various antique black wools for background, outer border, and hit-or-miss border
- ¼ yard *each* of three to five different beige and/or gray textured wools for the body of the horse and hit-or-miss border
- ¼ yard *each* of green, blue, red, brown, and mustard wool for hit-or-miss border
- 2 pieces, *each* 3" x 18", of darker beige and/or gray wool (darker than wool used for horse body) for the tail, ears, hooves, and mane
- 3" x 18" pieces of red, blue, and/or gold plaid cotton homespun as desired for hit-or-miss border
- 90 yards of black 3-ply wool yarn for whipping OR 3 yards of black binding tape

Drawing the Pattern

1. On the piece of backing, draw a 27" x 17" rectangle for the outer edge of the rug.
2. Enlarge the pattern on page 73 and make templates for the horse and the arch. Trace the arch template onto the backing.
3. Center the horse template inside the arch and trace around it.

Finished Size: 27" x 17"

Hints on Fabric Selection

- Textures in beige, taupe, and gray mixed together make a wonderful horse. You can also add some natural bulky wool yarn if you have some that goes with the woven wool you select. A coordinating color in a darker shade gives the mane, ears, hooves, and tail dimension.
- A mixture of antique black wools as a background makes the light horse stand out. Try dyeing some wool by using the formula on page 47.
- The hit-or-miss border includes the horse and background colors, in addition to the other wool and cotton homespuns. Pick wool scraps and cottons that go well together. You don't want anything that's too bright, and avoid too many different colors. Be sure to distribute the colors randomly throughout the border area.

4. To mark diagonal guidelines for the hit-or-miss border, start in the upper corners and draw a 45° line from each corner to the arched inside border line. Mark parallel lines around the border to keep your diagonals from going astray. The lines should meet in a V in the center of the top border.

Hooking Order

If you are going to use binding tape to finish this project, add it now or after step 2. See "Binding" on page 35.

1. Outline the body of the horse. Fill in the body with randomly selected strips of the wool you selected for the horse. Remember to include the eye in the color of your choice.

2. Outline and fill the mane, ears, and tail with the darker wool. The hooves will be only one line of a few loops.

3. Hook one row of antique black around the arched inside border line and one row around the horse. Fill in behind the horse with randomly pulled pieces of your antique black wool. Try meandering lines as I did to make the background interesting. Refer to "Meandering" on page 32 for further details if needed.

4. Hook one row of antique black on the outside edge of your pattern to create the outer border.

5. Now you're ready to hook the hit-or-miss border. Hit-or-miss borders have a scrappy, multicolor look and include the fabrics used in other parts of the rug. In order to keep the lines straight, it's best to work within the guidelines that you drew. Remember to step back and look at your border every now and then. You don't want your colors in a regimented order or bunched up in clumps of one color. You want a random, pleasing order.

6. Finish the rug according to the directions in "Finishing Your Rug" on page 35. The rug featured here was finished with black binding tape.

Tally Ho
One square equals
½".
Enlarge pattern 200%
and then 135%
(270% total)
to 27" x 17".

BIRD DOGG

Many old bed ruggs featured animals around the homestead, including the family dog. This black "dogg" is a hunting dog. With the little bird on his back, it makes you wonder how good a hunter he really is!

Materials

Yardages are generously estimated and based on 54"-wide wool fabric.

- Backing, 47" x 31" (51" x 35" if using a hoop)
- 1 yard of light to medium gray green wool for background
- 1 yard of gray green plaid wool for background (should blend with the lighter and darker gray green)
- ³⁄₄ yard of antique black wool for the dog, circles, corners, and outer border
- ¹⁄₂ yard of black, blue, purple, and green plaid wool for bird, circles, and corners
- ¹⁄₈ to ¹⁄₄ yard of blue wool for collar, circles, and corners
- ¹⁄₈ to ¹⁄₄ yard of dark gray green wool for background
- 8" x 18" piece of purple plaid wool for circles and corners
- 125 yards of black 3-ply wool yarn for whipping OR 4 yards of black binding tape

Drawing the Pattern

1. On the piece of backing, draw a 39" x 23" rectangle for the outer edge of the rug.
2. Enlarge the pattern on page 77 and make templates for the dog, his ear, the bird, the circles, and one of the corner arcs. Center the dog template on the background and trace. Allow room for the bird on his back. The top

Finished Size: 39" x 23"

Hints on Fabric Selection

- Using an antique black wool for the dog allows him to take center stage. If you decide to make him in another color, you may need to adjust the background colors to be sure he will stand out against them.
- The dark and medium gray green and gray green plaid background colors are variable. You need enough wool to fill in the background area with colors that work nicely with the plaid used in the bird.
- The bird's plaid can be any plaid you want. I used a plaid with black, blue, purple, and green. Choose two or three other colors from the plaid you select to use in the circles, dog collar, and corners.

of the bird's head should be 2" to 2¼" down from the top edge. Position and trace the bird.

3. Use the arc template as a guide to mark the corners; then draw successive arcs freehand.

4. Mark five circles using the circle templates or draw them freehand.

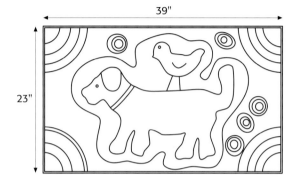

Hooking Order

If you are going to use binding tape to finish this project, add it now or after step 3. See "Binding" on page 35.

1. Outline and fill the dog. Don't forget his eye and collar.

2. Hook the bird and the bird's legs.

3. If you have two background colors, use the darker color (referred to as dark silver gray green in the materials list) and hook around the dog once. Then use the lighter color background wool to hook around the bird and dog. Continue with light wool until you have 2" to 2½" around the bird and dog. There will be areas where it will be more than 2½". Study the photograph of the rug to get an idea. You can draw an outline on your backing if you want.

4. Hook the circles randomly by using your accent colors.

5. Hook a few rows of the darker background color around the lighter background color.

6. Hook one row of antique black on the outside edge of your pattern to create the outer border.

7. Hook the corners by using all of the colors except the darker background color. Make the color combinations in each corner a little different.

8. Fill in the remainder of the background with the medium gray green.

9. Finish the rug according to the directions in "Finishing Your Rug" on page 35. The rug featured here was finished with black binding tape.

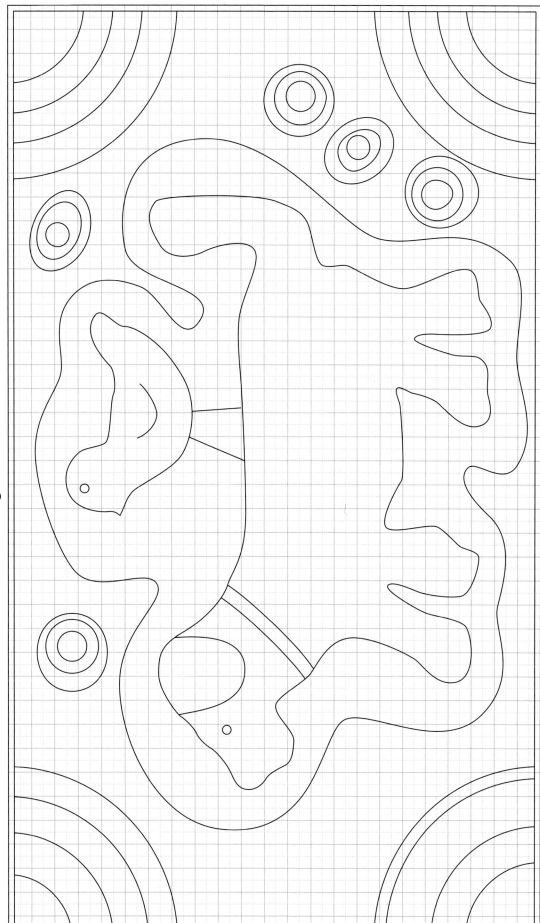

Bird Dogg
One square = ½".
Enlarge pattern
200% and then
200% (400% total)
to 39" x 23".

ANTIQUE PENNIES

This rug sits on my dining room table most of the year. I love the subtle colors and simplicity of the design. Antique pennies or circles aren't as easy as they look, but once you get the hang of hooking circles, it's fun. (See "Hooking Circles" on page 32 for helpful information.) This rug can be done in many different color schemes, and it's perfect if you want to use lots of scraps.

Materials

Yardages are generously estimated and based on 54"-wide wool fabric.

- Backing, 38" x 28" (42" x 32" if using a hoop)
- ³⁄₄ yard of buttermilk or golden wool for background
- ¹⁄₂ to ⁵⁄₈ yard of khaki drab wool for circles and border
- ¹⁄₂ to ⁵⁄₈ yard of antique black wool for circles and border
- ¹⁄₃ to ¹⁄₂ yard of old gold or honey mustard wool for circles and border
- 100 yards of old gold 3-ply wool yarn for whipping OR 3¹⁄₄ yards of old gold binding tape

Note: If you'd like to try your hand at dyeing wool, this is a good rug project for it. It uses antique black and khaki drab. Cushing-brand Old Gold and Olive Green would also make a wonderful pairing of colors for this rug.

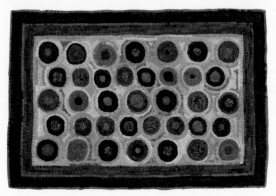

Finished Size: 30" x 20"

Hints on Fabric Selection

- Instead of buttermilk, make the background color antique black and use scraps for the circles. Use the same scraps in the border to frame the rug.

- The border is hooked in rows of three colors, starting inside and moving to the outside edge. The pattern is four rows of color 1, one row of color 2, four rows of color 3, and one row of color 2. For a different color combination from the one pictured, use four rows of gold, one row of red, four rows of antique black, and one row of red.

- A hit-or-miss (scrappy, multicolor look) border would also look good for this project. If you take that approach, consider the entire border as one unit rather than four narrow borders.

79

Drawing the Pattern

1. On the piece of backing, draw a 30" x 20" rectangle for the outer edge of the rug.

2. Draw the inside line of the border to measure 24½" x 14½".

3. There are two sizes of circles. Make templates from the patterns below. The larger circles go in the top, middle, and bottom rows, and there should be seven in each row. The smaller circles are in the two alternate rows; there are eight circles in each row. Space them so that there is enough room to hook background around each circle.

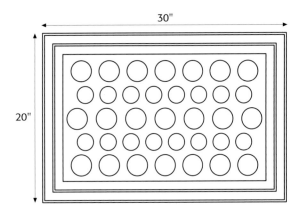

Hooking Order

If you are going to use binding tape to finish this project, add it now or after step 1. See "Binding" on page 35.

1. Work from the center of the pattern out. After you hook several circles, fill in some background behind them. Hook one row of buttermilk just to the inside of the inner border and continue filling in around the circles as they are hooked.

2. Hook the border in the following order, ending at the outside edge of your pattern: four rows of khaki drab next to the buttermilk, one row of old gold, four rows of antique black, and one row of old gold.

3. Finish the rug according to the directions in "Finishing Your Rug" on page 35. The rug featured here was finished using a binding tape.

Antique Pennies
Small Circle
Pattern is 100%.

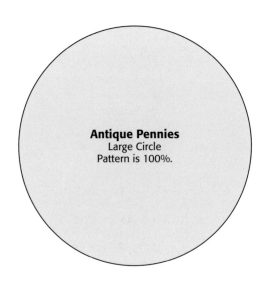

Antique Pennies
Large Circle
Pattern is 100%.

OLD HOMESTEAD

Rugs featuring the old homestead were a way of passing down a bit of history. They might have been as simple as the house by itself or include additional details such as the farm animals, pets, flowers, or even family members. Part of the charm of primitive designs is their lack of proportion. Note the size of the cat in this rug. Even though the cat is almost as wide as the house and as tall as the front door, he seems perfectly appropriate!

Materials

Yardages are generously estimated and based on 54"-wide wool fabric.

- Backing, 30" x 35" (34" x 39" if using a hoop)
- ½ yard of light to medium wool for background
- ½ yard of red-green-and-brown plaid wool for the tree and border
- ⅓ yard of green wool for the grass and border
- ⅓ yard of red wool for the house, chimney, and border
- ⅓ yard of reddish brown wool for the roof, door, and windows
- ¼ yard of gold wool for the stars and moon
- 10 yards of dark bulky wool yarn for the cat and tree trunk
- 99 yards *total* of 3-ply wool yarn in five to six colors for whipping OR 3 yards of binding tape

Finished Size: 22" x 27"

Hints on Fabric Selection

- I hooked this rug entirely with "as is" wool, meaning that the wool was not dyed or colored in any way and was used as is. You might want to consider doing the same.

- I used a small plaid of green and brown for the grass.

- The tree wool was a large plaid with brown, red, and green and gives the appearance of a tree with apples. If you can't find a plaid that gives the tree a fall look, try using a couple of different greens.

- Have fun choosing colors for the house, roof, doors, and moon to make it your own homestead. Then find a background color that harmonizes with all these colors. A heather or herringbone texture in an evening color might be perfect. I used a plaid that blended in well with the other wool used.

- I hooked the tree trunk and cat with wool yarn; you can substitute wool of your choice.

Drawing the Pattern

1. On the piece of backing, draw a 22" x 27" rectangle for the outer edge of the rug.

2. Draw the inside line of the border to measure 18" x 23".

3. Draw a wavy grass line about $2^{1}/_{2}$" up from the bottom inside border line. This line can range from 2" to $2^{3}/_{4}$".

4. Enlarge the patterns on page 84 and make templates for the cat, house, stars, moon, and tree.

5. Position the cat template on the left side and trace around it, leaving space for at least one row of background between the inside border line and the cat.

6. Place the tree template on the inside border line on the right and center the house between the cat and the tree. Trace the designs onto the backing.

7. Randomly place the stars and moon in the sky.

Hooking Order

If you are going to use binding tape to finish this project, add it now or after step 2. See "Binding" on page 35.

1. Outline the house and hook the roof, followed by the windows, door, and finally the house and chimney.

2. Hook the tree and then the cat.

3. Continue with the grass, moon, stars, and background.

4. Finish with the border. Work from the inside out with two rows of house red, two rows of grass green, and four rows of tree plaid.

5. Finish the rug according to the directions in "Finishing Your Rug" on page 35. This rug was finished using variegated wool yarn for whipping. The backing edge was folded over twice and whipped.

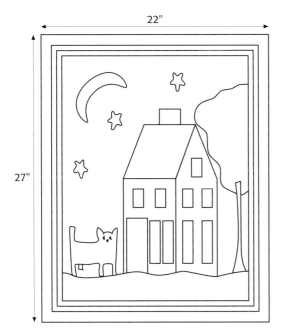

Old Homestead
One square = ½".
Enlarge pattern 200% and then
150% (300% total) to 22" x 27".

PRIMITIVE POSIES

Flowers were popular items in early rug designs. They were typically simple shapes without a lot of detail. I love big lollipop flowers hooked with textured wool and highlighted with plaid cotton homespun. This simple little rug offers lots of opportunities for using scraps. I suggest incorporating some cotton homespun into this one to experiment with a different fabric.

Materials

Yardages are generously estimated and based on 54"-wide wool fabric.

- Backing, 39" x 34" (43" x 37" if using a hoop)
- 1½ yards total of light to medium camel, caramel, or khaki wool for the background and border
- ½ yard total of three to five different brown textured wools for the basket and border
- ¼ yard of blue wool for flowers and border
- ¼ yard of red wool for flowers and border
- ¼ yard of green wool for leaves and border
- 1 fat quarter each of red plaid, gold plaid, and blue plaid cotton homespun for flowers
- 115 yards total of 3-ply wool yarn in six to eight colors for whipping OR 3½ yards of binding tape

Drawing the Pattern

1. On the piece of backing, draw a 31" x 26" rectangle for the outer edge of the rug.
2. Draw the inside line of the border to measure 26" x 21".
3. Enlarge the pattern on page 88 and make templates for the basket, flowers, and leaves.
4. Position the basket template in the center; there should be 2½" between the bottom of the basket and the inside bottom border line. Trace around the template.
5. Position the flower and leaf templates, using the master pattern on page 88 as a guide for the layout. The top of the center flower

Finished Size: 31" x 26"

Hints on Fabric Selection

- The background can be dyed wool or "as is" wool (wool that is not dyed or colored in any way and used as is). For visual interest, try to find a couple of similarly colored wools to hook randomly throughout the background.
- For the basket, mix several browns that go together. Look for a small check, her-ringbone, and/or brown plaid.
- The red, blue, and green areas were hooked with either dyed wool or a couple different pieces of "as is" wool.
- Cotton homespun fabric in small plaids with two or three colors in each plaid work best in the flowers. Different shades of plaids and a mix of cotton and wool give the flowers character.

should be 2" down from the inside border. Make sure there is room to hook background between the side flowers and the border. You want at least one row of background. Trace around the templates.

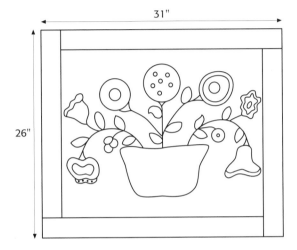

Hooking Order

If you are going to use binding tape to finish this project, add it now or after step 3. See "Binding" on page 35.

1. Hook the basket with the brown wools you selected. Vary the wool strips randomly to give the basket a woven look. When the basket is complete, hook a row of background color around it but remember to leave space for the stems along the upper edge.

2. Hook the center lollipop flower (flower D) next. Hook the little seeds in cotton homespun or in a different colored wool than the flower. Hook the center group of flowers (flowers C and E), stems, and leaves. Then follow with a row of background color.

3. Continue on with the other flowers (flowers A, B, F, and G), but work some background now and then so that you aren't left with all the background to do at one time.

4. Finally, hook the border. The border is a hit-or-miss border, which has a scrappy, multicolor look and includes fabrics used in other parts of the rug. However, before you begin, hook one row of basket browns to frame and separate the center from the border. Note the direction that the hit-or-miss border follows.

5. Finish the rug according to the directions in "Finishing Your Rug" on page 35. This rug has a whipped edge made by using six to eight different colored wool yarns.

The Flowers

Feel free to have fun and experiment with your own colors and fabrics in these flower shapes. To give you an idea how I mixed and matched cottons and wools, here are the colors and fabrics I used to hook the flowers in my rug. The flower letters (A-G) correspond with the letters on the patterns on page 88.

Flower A: Gold and red plaid cotton homespuns, green wool

Flower B: Blue plaid cotton homespun, red dyed wool

Flower C: Red dyed wool, blue plaid "as is" wool

Flower D: Outline in blue plaid "as is" wool, center in blue dyed wool, and yellow circles in gold plaid cotton homespun

Flower E: Red dyed wool, gold plaid cotton homespun

Flower F: Blue plaid cotton homespun, red dyed wool

Flower G: Blue plaid "as is" wool, green wool

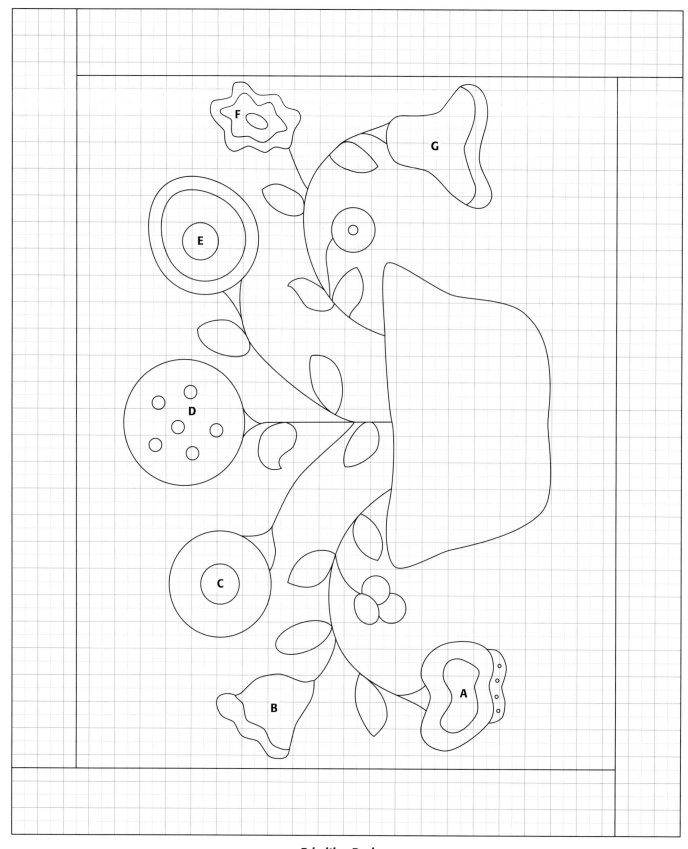

Primitive Posies
One square = ½".
Enlarge pattern 200% and then
180% (360% total) to 31" x 26".

SCRAP HAPPY

These cats and their bird friend are calling out to you to make them. However, this deceptively simple-looking rug may prove to be the most challenging project in this book. I wouldn't suggest doing it until you have done a few other rugs. If you are intimidated by hooking the background, cut several pieces of the wool, other fabrics, and yarn that you'll be using. Place them in a brown paper bag and randomly pull pieces to use. Sometimes you may not like what you pick. The limit is three tries. Then you must use what you pull. Remember—in the old days they didn't have the luxury of the options we have; they made do with what they had.

Materials

Yardages are generously estimated and based on 54"-wide wool fabric.

- Backing, 30" x 23" (34" x 27" if using a hoop)
- ½ yard of antique black wool for the cats, bird, and background
- ¼ yard of gray green wool for background
- ¼ yard of khaki wool for background
- ¼ yard of red wool for background
- 10 yards of dark brown (almost black) bulky wool yarn for the cats, bird, and background
- Scraps such as the following: cotton home-spun, army blanket, cotton velvet, wool felt, ultrasuede, and paisley shawl. Scraps can be as small as one strip to as many as ten strips. No large pieces are needed.
- 75 yards *total* of 3-ply wool yarn for whipping OR 2½ yards of binding tape

Drawing the Pattern

1. On the piece of backing, draw a 22" x 15" rectangle for the outer edge of the rug.
2. Make templates from the bird, cat, fish, and square patterns on pages 92–93.
3. Position and trace the cats facing each other in the bottom half of the rectangle. Leave enough room on the sides for the corner treatments and two bottom rows.
4. Center the bird template above the cats and trace around it. Again leave room for the three top rows and corners.
5. Draw the square and the fish shape in the approximate area shown on the illustration on page 91.

Finished Size: 22" x 15"

Hints on Fabric Selection

- Use several different blacks, gray greens, khakis, and reds to make up the yardage required. The colors should be similar to one another but different enough to create interest.
- In collecting the other fabrics, pick colors that blend or coordinate with the wool you choose. If you have a true khaki, don't throw in white wool yarn. It will jump out and not be pleasing.

6. The outside edge has one complete row hooked around it. From there draw your corner quarter circles. Vary them in design. Note that the top of the rug has three horizontal

rows between the corner quarter circles if you count the outermost row, and the bottom has two horizontal rows.

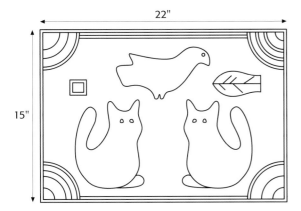

22"

15"

Hooking Order

If you are going to use binding tape to finish this project, add it now or after step 3. See "Binding" on page 35.

1. Start with the cats. Use several different blacks, browns, wool yarn, and/or cotton homespun. Try using strips from the army blanket for the cat eyes.

2. Hook the bird. Give life to it by adding some black that has a hint of red or purple to it.

3. Now the challenging part begins. First, make sure you work in small areas. Outline the cats twice and then follow with the two bottom rows. Next concentrate on the space between the cats.

4. Continue working in small areas. Vary your colors, your materials, and the shapes you choose to hook. Occasionally step away from your work. This part isn't easy and you may need to make some adjustments as you go.

5. Try very hard not to have blobs of color or spots that immediately draw your eye. Relax, play with it, and have fun.

6. Finish the rug according to the directions in "Finishing Your Rug" on page 35. The rug featured here was finished with cording and black 3-ply wool yarn.

The Story of This Rug

Scrap Happy was thrown together in a hurry. I was invited at the last minute to participate in a weekend workshop on Cape Cod. There was a cancellation and I was the lucky person to fill the slot. I was told to bring a pattern and various fabrics in addition to wool.

I was inspired by a rug I had seen in the book *American Hooked and Sewn Rugs: Folk Art Underfoot* by Joel Kopp and Kate Kopp. The original rug had a big dog and two large birds. I designed my rug with the two cats and a bird and kept the size small in case I wasn't happy with the results.

The hunt for fabrics other than wool began. I have been a quilter for a long time, so I hit my cotton stash first. I pulled out cotton homespuns and some wool felt. Then I threw in some bulky wool yarn and decided that was the best I could do on such short notice.

At the workshop, other people contributed a piece of army blanket, red velvet for the bird's eye, a piece of blue-black ultrasuede that was used in one of the cats, and a piece of paisley shawl; the instructor gave us each a piece of vintage wool fabric from the late 1800s. Once I got going on this rug I didn't want it to end. It was so much fun. Scrappy rugs don't appeal to everyone, but for those who are drawn to them, it's like putting together the ultimate jigsaw puzzle.

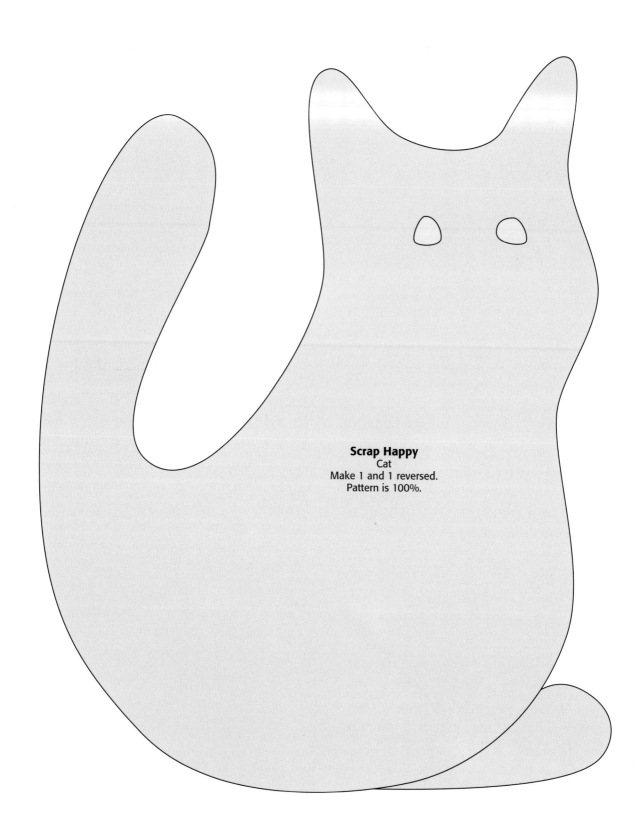

Scrap Happy
Cat
Make 1 and 1 reversed.
Pattern is 100%.

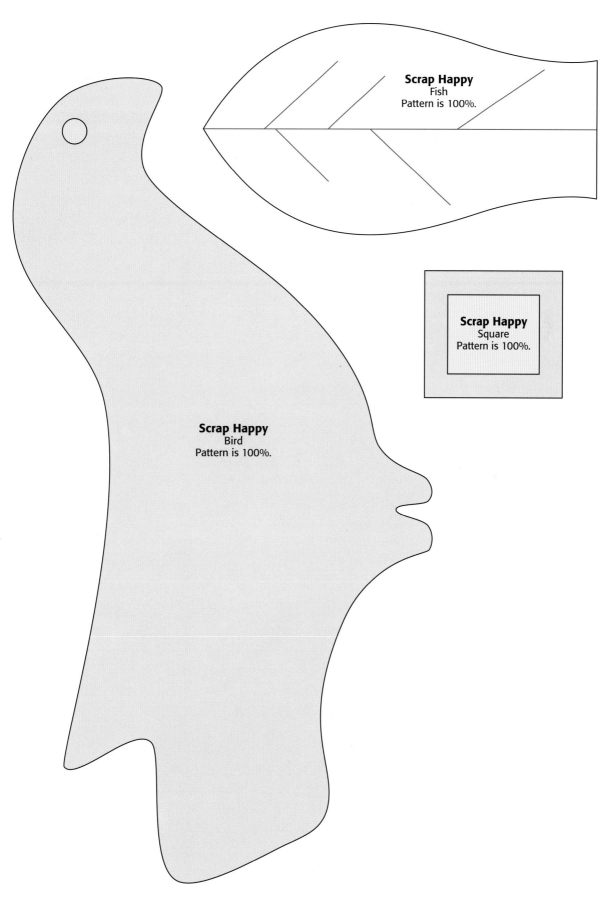

Scrap Happy
Fish
Pattern is 100%.

Scrap Happy
Square
Pattern is 100%.

Scrap Happy
Bird
Pattern is 100%.

RESOURCES

Now that I have you "hooked," you're going to want to read more about rug-hooking history and look at pictures of wonderful, old hooked rugs. The following books are very informative and have many great color photographs. I've also included a list of suppliers for rug-hooking equipment. These are companies I have dealt with over the years and are good places to start.

Of the three magazines I've listed, only *Rug Hooking Magazine* can be found at bookstores. The others are by subscription only. All of them contain great articles, color photographs and illustrations, and extensive lists of suppliers, camps, and teachers.

Books on Rug Hooking

Beatty, Alice, and Mary Sargent. *Basic Rug Hooking.* Harrisburg, Pa: Stackpole Books, 1990.

Boswell, Thom. *The Rug Hook Book.* New York: Sterling Publishing Co., Inc., 1992.

Carroll, Barbara, and Emma Lou Lais. *American Primitive Hooked Rugs: A Primer for Re-creating Antique Rugs.* Kennebunkport, Maine: Wildwood Press, 1999.

Kopp, Joel, and Kate Kopp. *American Hooked and Sewn Rugs: Folk Art Underfoot.* New York: E. P. Dutton & Co. Inc., 1975.

Linsley, Leslie. *Hooked Rugs: An American Folk Art.* New York: Clarkson N. Potter, Inc., 1992.

Turbayne, Jessie A. *Hooked Rug Treasury.* Atglen, Pa: Schiffer Publishing Ltd., 1997.

————. *Hooked Rugs: History and the Continuing Tradition.* West Chester, Pa: Schifffer Publishing Ltd., 1991.

————. *The Hooker's Art: Evolving Designs in Hooked Rugs.* Atglen, Pa: Schiffer Publishing Ltd., 1993.

Books on Dyeing

Lais, Emma Lou, and Barbara Carroll. *Antique Colours for Primitive Rugs: Formulas Using Cushing's Acid Dyes.* Kennebunkport, Maine: W. Cushing & Company, 1996.

Wiles, Laurilyn. *Vermont Folk Rugs: Dyeing to Get Primitive Colors on Wool.* Hinesburg, Vt: Vermont Folk Rugs.

Magazines

Association of Traditional Hooking Artists (ATHA)
Nancy Martin, Membership Chairperson
1360 Newman Avenue
Seekonk, MA 02771
1-508-399-8230

Rug Hooking Magazine
1300 Market Street, Suite 202
Lemoyne, PA 17043
1-800-233-9055

The Wool Street Journal
312 North Custer
Colorado Springs, CO 80903
1-888-RUG-LOOP

Suppliers of Cutters, Frames, Dyes, and Wool

Braid Aid
PO Box 603
Pembroke, MA 02359
1-781-826-6091
www.braid-aid.com

The Dorr Mill Store
PO Box 88
Guild, NH 03754
1-800-846-DORR
www.dorrmillstore.com

Harry M. Fraser Company
PO Box 939
Stoneville, NC 27048
1-336-573-9830
www.fraserrugs.com

The Needle Nook
Donna McDowell
100 E. Main Street
Ligonier, PA 15658
724-238-7874

Rigby Precision Products
PO Box 158
Bridgton, ME 04009
1-207-647-5679

Townsend Industries Inc.
PO Box 97
Altoona, IA 50009
1-877-868-3544

W. Cushing & Company
PO Box 351
Kennebunkport, ME 04046
1-800-626-7847
www.wcushing.com

The Wool Studio
706 Brownsville Road
Sinking Spring, PA 19608
1-610-678-5448
www.thewoolstudio.com

BIBLIOGRAPHY

Beatty, Alice, and Mary Sargent. *Basic Rug Hooking.* Harrisburg, Pa: Stackpole Books, 1990.

Bishop, Robert, William Secord and Judith Reiter Weissman. *Quilts, Coverlets, Rugs and Samplers.* New York: Alfred A. Knopf, 1982.

Kent, William Winthrop. *Hooked Rug Design.* Springfield, Mass.: The Pond-Ekberg Co. Publishers, 1949.

———. *The Hooked Book.* New York: Tudor Publishing Company, 1937.

Ketchum, William C., Jr. *Hooked Rugs: A Historical and Collector's Guide: How To Make Your Own.* New York and London, England: Harcourt Brace Jovanovich, 1976.

Kimmel, Gerry, and Linda Brannock. *Free Spirit.* Liberty, Mo.: Red Wagon, 1992.

Kopp, Joel, and Kate Kopp. *American Hooked and Sewn Rugs: Folk Art Underfoot.* New York: E. P. Dutton & Co. Inc., 1975.

Moshimer, Joan. *The Complete Book of Rug Hooking.* New York: Dover Publications, 1989.

Ries, Estelle H. *The American Arts Library: American Rugs.* Cleveland, N.Y.: The World Publishing Company, 1950.

Rex, Stella Hay. *Practical Hooked Rugs.* New York: Prentice-Hall, Inc., 1949.

ABOUT THE AUTHOR

Pat Cross lives in Charlottesville, Virginia, with her husband, Tom, and their two cats, Emma and Scout—also known as the "girls." She has been hooking rugs for twelve years. During this time she has developed a unique style that makes her primitive, scrappy rugs look like antiques. She has attended more than a dozen rug camps, is active in many rug-hooking organizations, has been teaching for over five years, won a blue ribbon at the Kentucky State Fair for a hooked rug, and has been published in *Rug Hooking Magazine*.

Pat's love for rug hooking grew from her mother's love of antiques; her mother also did needlework and made braided rugs. When Pat first watched her college housemother hook rugs, she became fascinated by the art. Frequent moves throughout her life have made her appreciate tradition, history, and the need people have to make their home safe and warm. She translates this into her unique designs that have that scrappy look of antique, primitive hooked rugs.